HISPANICS IN AMERICAN POLITICS

The Search for Political Power

Maurilio E. Vigil

UNIVERSITY
PRESS OF
AMERICA

Lanham • New York • London

British Cataloging in Publication Information Available

Library of Congress Cataloging-in-Publication Data

Vigil, Maurilio E., 1941-
  Hispanics in American politics.

  1. Hispanic Americans—Politics and government.
I. Title.
E184.S75V54 1987   324.973'008968   87-1753
ISBN 0-8191-6118-7 (alk. paper)
ISBN 0-8191-6119-5 (pbk. : alk. paper)

All University Press of America books are produced on acid-free
paper which exceeds the minimum standards set by the National
Historical Publication and Records Commission.

For
Melecio and Juanita
and all of our ancestors whose
legacy we share.

"En la union nace la fuerza."

An old Hispanic proverb.

iii

ACKNOWLEDGMENT

In writing this book I have received support from the Institute of Research at New Mexico Highlands University for typing of the manuscript. I am especially grateful for the contribution of my Graduate Assistant, Milane Egert, who extended great effort in typing and editing earlier drafts of the manuscript and Mrs. Jean Greer who typed the final draft. I also appreciate the help offered by the staff of Donnelly Library for their assistance in securing some sources of information.

A word about terminology used in referring to the groups in this study is appropriate. As will be explained later the all-encompassing term "Hispanics" is used purposely because of the desire to explore the legitimacy of the broader "Hispanic" minority over particular Hispanic subgroups such as Spanish, Mexican, Cuban or Puerto Rican Americans. The term "Hispanic" is an adjective. As a rule, in translation when there is an appropriate noun in the foreign language such as "Hispano," it is most appropriate to use it in referring to the group. However, the popularization of the term "Hispanics" by the U.S. Census Bureau, social scientists and writers in the media have contributed to its common usage which is followed here.

CONTENTS

ILLUSTRATIONS

INTRODUCTION

If a book on Hispanics in American politics had been written ten or even twenty years ago it might well have been dismissed as a superficial or contrived effort to create a hypothetical minority out of various diverse groups. It most certainly would have been rejected by any one group of Hispanics, especially the Mexican-Americans, who were the most parochial sub-group in their ethnic affiliations due to such developments as the Chicano movement.

Indeed, the plethora of books that appeared in the 1960's and 1970's on Mexican-Americans especially, but also on Puerto Ricans and Cubans, reflected a new interest in these heretofore "forgotten Americans," who had emerged as a vital new force in American politics.(1) Consistently, however, the authors of these many books were careful to identify the specific Hispanic group which was the focus of their study. They then proceeded to relate the historical background, political culture, political activity, leaders, organizations and accomplishments of that group in American politics.

Many of the reasons for that separate and segmented treatment remain as powerful and valid today as they were ten years ago. The Hispanics are, as most textbooks tell us,(2) a very diverse group. Hispanics are not only diverse in national origin and economic status but also geographically dispersed across the country. The historical experience and political development of each of the three main subgroups--Mexican-Americans, Cubans and Puerto Ricans--are as different from one another as from other American ethnic groups. In fact, in comparing similarities and differences among the various Hispanic groups, one may be more impressed by the differences than by the unifying characteristics of language, surnames and common Spanish origin.

This book's premise, that Hispanic groups in this country have reached the point where they must accept being categorized as a single ethnic group, is controversial and will not be easily accepted. The effort here is to consider the realities and possibilities of conceptualizing Hispanics as a viable political group in American politics. The book includes a summary of the themes, events, personalities, organizations and activities which have shaped Hispanics' long and eventful history in the United States. Knowledgeable readers will discover quickly that some topic, personality, event or organization has been omitted. However, limited resources have necessitated compressing the volume to the most important topics which has meant that we have had to be very selective in determining what would be included and in drawing upon general trends rather than specific events. The overall effort has been to produce a first work on Hispanics in American politics which can serve as the basis for those interested in studying the subject. Hopefully this initial venture will generate sufficient interest and demand for a more extensive effort.

The Case For Hispanic Politics

There are several compelling reasons for considering the realities and possibilities of such a designation as Hispanics in American politics. For one thing, the term Hispanics is one that has caught on in the popular media, television, radio, newspapers, and popular magazines, all of which increasingly portray the Hispanic rather than the more particular group. Expanded spheres of communication such as cable and network television have created more of a "national" community in this country. Within that context, the Hispanics are joined as a sub-community of the American people and even with the larger Hispanic world community by SIN, the Spanish language network. Such communication has provided a window through which different Hispanic groups, once shut off, are now capable of observing each other and the similarities in their cultures. Increased use of the term Hispanic by the U.S. Census Bureau and other government agencies has also helped to popularize the concept of Hispanics as a homogeneous minority group. The convenience of referring to this all-encompassing term has, moreover, become popular among national politicians. In their search for identifiable voting blocs, presidential candidates have been impressed by the population numbers offered by Hispanics, often counted as the nation's second largest minority. New Mexico Governor Toney Anaya and his proposed Hispanic Force '84, for example, sought ways to establish linkages that would consolidate the diverse segments into a cohesive political group. From a purely practical perspective, one must consider the impressive number of Hispanic Americans. Counted together, Hispanics make up 14.6 million people or 6.4 percent of the U.S. population. Counted as distinct subgroups, they diminish into less significant numbers. Mexican-Americans, the largest group, comprise 8.7 million people (3.8 percent of the U.S. population); Puerto Ricans (2 million) and Cubans

(800,000) each make up less than 1 percent of the U.S. population. The remainder, made up of Hispanics from other Central and South American countries and Spain, number about 3 million, or about 1 percent of the U.S. population.

Finally, counting any racial group as a minority is a hypothetical contrivance that denies the inherent geographical, ideological, economic, class and religious differences that characterize even the homogeneous group. Thus, the Mexican-American subgroup is in itself characterized by internal regional and economic differences that negate its status as a homogeneous minority group. Given these conditions, then, recognition of any group as a minority is a matter of perspective. If considering Mexican-Americans as a minority group in the Southwest has inherent advantage from one perspective, then one can equally argue from another perspective that Hispanics can be perceived as a national minority group for similar advantage.

Consequently, the effort of this book will be to evaluate and analyze the evolving role of Hispanics in American politics. It will attempt to review the historical experiences and political cultures of the various groups comprising the Hispanic population, their leadership, organizations and levels of participation in politics, and to speculate on the prospects for Hispanics in American politics. It is important to note that the analysis of the Hispanic group, like any other, constitutes an effort to analyze the activities of the component parts which collectively make up the whole. Thus, analysis of any one group will be done from the wider global perspective of its importance not only for the subgroup, but for the larger Hispanic community.

A Demographic Profile and Political Prospects

Considered from this wider perspective, Hispanics are potentially one of the most important ethnic minority groups in the country. Hispanics are the second largest ethnic minority at 14.6 million people (6.4 percent of the U.S. population). Twenty-seven million Blacks, twelve percent of the U.S. population, are the largest ethnic minority. More important from a political perspective is the fact that Hispanics, already a young population (with a median age 23.2 as compared to 31.6 for white Americans), are the fastest growing group, with an increase of 61 percent between 1970 and

1980 compared to only 8 percent for white Americans. Hispanics also have the highest birth rate. A U.S. Census report showed that Hispanic women average 97.9 births per 1,000 compared to 68.1 for white women and 83.6 for black women. Projections suggest that if the current Hispanic growth of population continues they will number over 25 million persons by the year 2000 and 47 million by the year 2020, thus displacing Blacks as the largest ethnic minority.(3) The number if Hispanics counted in the U.S. population could also increase abruptly if the proposal to grant amnesty to the many illegal aliens in this country is adopted. Indeed, the compromise version of the Simpson-Mazzoli Bill passed by the U.S. House of Representatives in 1984 called for the granting of amnesty to illegal aliens residing in the United States. Some observers estimate that as many as 7.4 million uncounted Hispanic aliens now reside in the U.S.(4) Moreover, considering economic conditions in Mexico and the political turmoil in Central America, it is likely that the tide of illegal immigration to the United States will continue. Although the U.S. government has shown some intransigence in addressing the issue of the exact legal status of these "aliens," their continued residence here will necessitate that the U.S. eventually integrate them.

The geographic distribution of Hispanics in the United States is another factor to consider. Were the group dispersed equally throughout the country, they would not pose a viable political force. However, Hispanics are heavily concentrated in ten states, seven of which are among the country's largest in population and electoral votes. Table I illustrates the ten states with the heaviest concentration of Hispanic population. Hispanics make up 14.2 percent of the voting age population of Texas with 26 electoral votes; 8.7 percent in California with 45 electoral votes; 6.3 percent in New York with 41 electoral votes; and 4.5 and 4.1 percent in New Jersey and Florida respectively, each with 17 electoral votes. Hispanics make up larger proportions of the voting age populations of New Mexico (32.3 percent), Arizona (11.5 percent) and Colorado (9.4 percent) with a total of 17 electoral votes among them. Overall, Hispanics thus form a significant minority that can serve as a critical swing vote in the ten states listed which possess a total of 210 electoral votes (270 are needed for Presidential election).

Not only are Hispanics concentrated in specific states, but they are heavily concentrated in metropoli-

4

TABLE I

HISPANIC POPULATION AND POPULATION OF VOTING AGE:
TEN MOST POPULOUS HISPANIC STATES

STATE	HISPANIC POPULATION	PERCENT HISPANIC	HISPANICS OF VOTING AGE	PERCENT HISPANIC
CALIFORNIA	4,544,000	19.1	1,501,000	8.7
TEXAS	2,986,000	20.0	1,414,000	14.2
NEW YORK	1,659,000	9.4	811,000	6.3
FLORIDA	858,000	8.8	313,000	4.2
NEW MEXICO	477,000	36.6	286,000	32.3
NEW JERSEY	492,000	6.6	242,000	4.5
ARIZONA	441,000	16.2	222,000	11.5
COLORADO	340,000	11.7	196,000	9.4
ILLINOIS	636,000	5.5	189,000	2.3
MICHIGAN	162,000	1.7	74,000	1.1

Source: Table developed from data of the U.S. Census Bureau, Statistical Abstract of the United States, 1985, 105th Edition (Washington, D.C. U.S. Government Printing Office, 1985, p. 35 along with data provided by the Southwest Voter Registration and Education Project.

tan areas. As shown in Table II, 2.1 million Hispanics (mostly Mexican-Americans) live in Los Angeles, where they make up 28 percent of the population; 1.5 million Hispanics (mostly Puerto Rican) live in New York where they comprise 16.4 percent of the population; 580,000 live in Miami (mostly Cuban) where they make up 35 percent of the population; and 580,000 live in Chicago (mostly Mexican-American) where they make up 8.2 percent of the population. San Antonio with its 481,000 Hispanics (mostly Mexican-American) has the highest proportion of Hispanics. These figures explain why Hispanics as a group have joined Blacks as the two most sought after ethnic voting blocs in American presidential elections.

Equally important to their potential impact in national politics is the day-to-day impact which Hispanics can have in the politics of their ten states, in the governorships, the state legislatures and in county, municipal and school board politics.

Juxtaposed to these impressive figures, however, is the harsh reality that even with intensive voter registration drives launched by groups such as the Southwest Voter Registration Education Project (SWVREP), Hispanics as a whole have had comparatively low levels of political participation. In 1983, for example, only 58 percent of the Mexican-Americans were registered to vote as compared to 74 percent of the Anglos. In common with other minority groups, especially Black Americans, Hispanics have faced numerous obstacles to political participation. Included are literacy and language tests, poll taxes, the white primary and intimidation by dominant white groups or organizations like the Ku Klux Klan. The language barrier was addressed by reforms such as the Voting Rights Act of 1970, which required that ballots be printed in both English and Spanish in districts where at least 5 percent of the registered voters are Spanish-speaking. The 1970 Voting Rights Act and subsequent amendments have thus helped remove some of the barriers to Hispanic voting. It is expected that renewed interest by the major parties in capturing the Hispanic vote, registration drives by parties and groups like SWVREP and greater political socialization of Hispanic voters to American politics will reverse the trend of low participation.

Obviously, the extent of political influence that can be achieved by Hispanics will depend in large part on the success of registering voters and getting them

TABLE II

TOP TWENTY SMSA'S[1] IN HISPANIC POPULATION

RANK	SMSA[1]	1980 HISPANIC POPULATION	PERCENT HISPANIC	PREDOMINANT HISPANIC GROUP
1.	Los Angeles, Ca	2,066,103	27.6	80% M-A
2.	New York, NY	1,493,148	16.4	60% PR
3.	Miami, Fl	580,994	35.7	70% Cuban
4.	Chicago, Il	580,609	8.2	64% M-A
5.	San Antonio, Tx	481,511	44.9	93% M-A
6.	Houston, Tx	424,093	14.6	88% M-A
7.	San Francisco/Oakland, Ca	351,698	10.8	54% M-A
8.	El Paso, Tx	297,001	61.9	95% M-A
9.	Riverside/San Bernardino, Ca	290,280	18.6	87% M-A
10.	Anaheim/Santa Ana, Ca	286,339	14.8	81% M-A
11.	San Diego, Ca	275,177	14.8	83% M-A
12.	Dallas-Fort Worth, Tx	249,614	8.4	90% M-A
13.	McAllen-Pharr, Tx	230,212	81.3	96% M-A
14.	San Jose, Ca	226,611	17.5	78% M-A
15.	Phoenix, Az	199,003	13.2	89% M-A
16.	Denver, Co	173,773	10.7	63% M-A
17.	Albuquerque, NM	164,200	36.1	Note 2
18.	Brownsville/Harlingen, Tx	161,654	77.1	86% M-A
19.	Corpus Christi, Tx	158,119	48.5	96% M-A
20.	Fresno, Ca	150,790	29.3	94% M-A

Source: Caminos Research and Marketing, appearing in Hispanic Conventioneers, 1985, p. 14.

1. Refers to Standard Metropolitan Statistical Area.
2. In Albuquerque most Hispanics are Mexican-American, though they label themselves as Other Hispanic.

out to vote. It will also depend on the degree of unity that can be manifested by the group in voting as a cohesive bloc. This problem presents a formidable challenge to Hispanic organizations and leaders because the various subgroups, as indicated before, have had different political orientations and are located in different regions of the country. Politically, Cubans have been more conservative and Republican Party-oriented while Mexican-Americans and Puerto Ricans have been more liberal and supportive of the Democratic Party. Hispanics have also lacked a single unifying issue, such as civil rights, which solidified the Black community.

Nonetheless, common language, Spanish surnames and Spanish cultural antecedents might serve as possible bonds that could be utilized effectively by national political parties, candidates and Hispanic leaders and organizations to weld together a formidable coalition of Hispanics. There are, after all, many social, economic and educational problems that are common to all Hispanics.

Invariably, the central element to any success which will be achieved politically by Hispanics as a group is group consciousness. It is the one ingredient which has welded the Blacks into the most powerful ethnic group in the United States and it is what is needed by Hispanics. Although each of the Hispanic subgroups has achieved a certain level of group con-sciousness as Mexican, Cuban or Puerto Rican Americans, their broader viability as a Hispanic group requires greater consciousness as such.

In the past Hispanics, like Blacks and Indians, have been characterized by negative self-images. Discrimination, prejudice and domination in American society created beliefs and attitudes among Hispanics that caused them to feel inadequate, unequal, incompe-tent and inferior.

In more recent times, however, Hispanics (like other minorities) have undergone important changes. They have achieved a higher level of awareness of their culture, history and values and have found strengths in these cultures. This awareness has contributed to a higher sense of ethnic pride which has enhanced the group's sense of political efficacy or ability to influence the American social and political environ-ment.

8

Historian Page Smith has called this new awareness "Peoplehood." Peoplehood, writes Smith,

...is a particular kind of self-definition whereby masses or wards of the public seek to achieve an identity and a power of their own...the definition comes out of the mass; it can never come from outside from well-intentioned liberals, benefactors, reformers, philosophers, psychologists, sociologists...the dependent group in the process of defining itself, of creating itself, of sparking itself into life, draws on remarkable new sources of energy and releases these into the world.(5)

Ultimately, Smith says, the group becomes "electrified" or "plugged in" to history, thinking that they also are capable of making history. This is the kind of dynamic force that Hispanics are capable of, and are literally on the threshold of, if they can achieve the necessary level of group consciousness.

Chapter Organization and Plan of This Book

The chapters that follow will attempt to treat the most important themes pertaining to American Hispanics in a systematic fashion. Each chapter is organized around a specific theme that is uniquely important but is related to others in subsequent chapters in providing a complete view of Hispanic politics.

Chapter I reviews various theoretical approaches to the study of minorities in American politics and presents an eclectic model that applies to Hispanics in American politics. Chapter II presents historical sketches of the main Hispanic subgroups--Mexican-Americans, Cubans, Puerto Ricans--and others with emphasis on their current situation in American life. Chapter III summarizes the developing voting patterns of Hispanics in national, state and local politics as well as the ideological, partisan and issue orientations of the Hispanic vote. Chapter IV focuses on Hispanics in national office including their role in Congress and as appointees in the Executive branch of government. Chapter V explores Hispanic involvement in state and local government with particular emphasis on the most successful Hispanic politicians at those levels. Chapter VI reviews the many Hispanic organizations and discusses the various activities of the most prominent ones. The final chapter discusses potential strategies and future prospects for Hispanics given the trends discussed in the preceding chapters.

Summary

This section has presented the "best case" scenario for "Hispanics in American Politics." Although the differences which have kept Hispanics apart as separate subgroups are as compelling today as they ever were, several equally powerful forces have emerged to underscore the need for a single Hispanic identity. Despite different sociopolitical and historical experiences, the powerful magnet of Hispanic culture and language have served as a common bond for Hispanics. Increased reference to "Hispanics" by the media, politicians and government agencies and the sheer advantage of numbers serve as powerful pressures toward political integration of all Hispanics. The purpose of this book is to evaluate and analyze the prospects for this evolving Hispanic group in American politics.

CHAPTER I

HISPANICS IN AMERICAN POLITICS:
A THEORETICAL APPROACH

Although the United States has always been a diverse, pluralistic society with a great assortment of racial, religious, ethnic, economic and ideological differences among its people, this has not always been reflected in philosophical characterizations of American society. Voters have always made political choices as members of a particular ethnic or other group; although these groups of people have maintained fairly consistent voting patterns over a period of time, there has been a reluctance to recognize such voting patterns. Walter Kantowicz points out that "although ethnicity formed the basis of party politics through much of American history, it was most visible in the realm of big-city boss politics. Since the middle of the 19th century, the majority of immigrants to America settled in the cities where the representative of a political machine usually introduced them to American politics."(1) The reason for this reluctance to recognize such diversity on ethnic voting is that it runs counter to certain propositions about the homogeneity of American culture and life.

Traditional philosophical characterizations of American life depict a very homogeneous society and culture. Americans, it is assumed, embrace a single, if vague concept of democracy. Any deviation from the popular conception of democracy is seen as a challenge or threat and is labeled "un-American." Similarly, traditional assumptions of Americanism stress a single identity. Other than emphasizing White-Anglo-Saxon-Protestant (WASP) and English language ideals, the exact identity of an American remains vague. Nevertheless, the call for ethnic Americans to forget their ethnic or cultural origins as a way of becoming "American" has been clear and insistent.

Such calls for Americanism have caused the true nature of America's ethnic pluralism or heterogeneity to be clouded by a myth of American homogeneity. Teddy Roosevelt reflected the common intolerance for ethnic differences in voting when he said, "We have no room for any people who do not act and vote simply as Americans and nothing else."

Such attitudes have been interwoven into a systematic ethic which argues that ethnics are no longer

ethnics but are all "Americans." Sophisticated socio-
logical theories such as assimilation and the melting
pot have been advanced to validate the logic of one
single homogeneous American culture.

For some time however, social scientists have been
challenging both the singular democratic theory and the
concept of an American culture. As Michael Levy and
Marv Kramer have pointed out, "Our efforts have proven
to us, persuasively, that the hyphenated Americans do
vote as ethnic blocs, and that, at least, political
assimilation has not occurred...past national affiliations speak eloquently at the polls and retain their
complex interrelationships."(2)

The first task that faces the social scientist who
seeks to study one particular ethnic group such as
Hispanics in American politics is to place that group
in the context of traditional and modern conceptions of
democratic political theory and the dynamics of American culture and intergroup relations.

The following discussion will first explore
democratic theories and then theories of intergroup
relations in an effort to develop an eclectic model for
understanding the place of Hispanics in American
society.

Although political theorists have evolved many
variations of American democratic theory, it is possible to summarize them under three distinct
categories--traditional democratic theory, elitism and
pluralism. All of these theories seek to explain the
distribution of values in society, the legitimacy of
the political system, and the political behavior that
is appropriate among its people.

<u>Traditional</u> <u>democratic</u> <u>theory</u> places great stress
on individual freedom and equality. The emphasis is on
direct participatory democracy where all the people are
involved in directing the affairs of government. The
theory has been found wanting in American politics; in
fact the vast majority of American citizens remain
apart from governing. In practical application, as Levy
and Kramer point out, "such a philosophy falls short of
its internally consistent theoretical underpinnings and
democracy by proxy becomes a psychological fraud as the
individual who is spoken for by the large pressure
group has himself little voice within the rigid group
framework."(3) <u>Elite</u> <u>theory</u> argues that only a few
govern American society. The elite, comprised of a

few business, government and military leaders, sit at the top of the pyramid of power and determine public policy. This theory is also lacking in that it assumes a consensus and frequent interaction among the elites that is difficult to document. Pluralism contends that power in American society is fragmented among different institutions, levels of government and private sectors of society. Many different interest groups and power sources are locked in conflict and competition for influence in decision-making, and public policy is the temporary equilibrium reached through compromise among the competing groups. This latter theory of pluralism lends itself most readily to the analysis of ethnic groups in American politics, if one regards the ethnic group as one of those potential sources of influence.

Students of ethnic politics have also been interested in developing theories that apply to the acculturation or adaptation of ethnic groups to the American system. It is useful to review some of these theories and their application in the case of Hispanics in American politics.

Internal Colonialism

Some writers have suggested that the internal colonialism model(4) best explains minorities in American politics. This view suggests that the U.S. government has treated minorities in a paternalistic fashion. All Hispanic groups, Blacks, and Indians were treated as conquered colonies by subordinating them and forcing them to accept the values and the culture of the dominant society. Relegated to a second-class status, these groups were victims of discrimination, prejudice, economic and political subordination.

Anglo Conformity or Assimilation

This model, a variation of the first, suggests that American society has forced or pressured minority groups to disassociate from their antecedent cultures and to adopt attitudes, lifestyles and culture of the dominant society. The assumption is that eventually all ethnics become "American" through this process of assimilation.

Melting Pot

This ideology, given impetus by the observations of Israel Zangwill and Farmer Crevecour, is a minority ideology which suggests that the United States is a population mixture of many different cultures and nationalities. The different nationalities and their cultures have been melted down in the cauldron of the American cities and the product has been a unique blend--an American culture. The theory has been criticized by racial minorities, the unmeltables who have seen the American city more as a "pressure cooker."

Cultural Pluralism, a more recent theory, has found vogue among activist minorities. This theory presents American society as a "patchwork" of different nationalities and cultural groups. This is similar to a tossed salad in which the various ingredients retain their distinct identity and flavor though comprising a part of the larger identity.

In summary, no single social theory is appropriate in itself, since all of the theories are valid to a degree. It is true that minorities have historically been subordinated and victims of prejudice and discrimination and have been socially and politically segregated. It is true also that they have been forced to acculturate to Anglo-American values and cultural norms such as the English language. It is, however, also true that American culture represents diverse influences of different groups as the melting pot theory would suggest. Finally, it is also possible to distinguish some groups which have retained their ethnic identities as suggested by the cultural pluralists.

Employing an eclectic application of the various social and political theories presented above, it is possible to conclude that American society is a pluralistic society made up of a wide and diverse assortment of economic, regional, religious, ideological, ethnic and racial groups which wield varying levels of influence in politics. These groups are locked in competition or conflict with each other and the demands and expectations generated by these groups (as shown in Figure 1) form the inputs that the political system transforms into outputs or public policies. Public policies are temporary decisions based on the relative strength of the groups and the natural tendency toward compromise. American government thus serves as the referee and arbiter of conflict. The political system has many access points and contains many institutions that can be made to respond by the specific interest or minority group.

How does this model account for the traditional

FIGURE I

ETHNIC GROUPS IN AMERICAN POLITICS: A PARADIGM

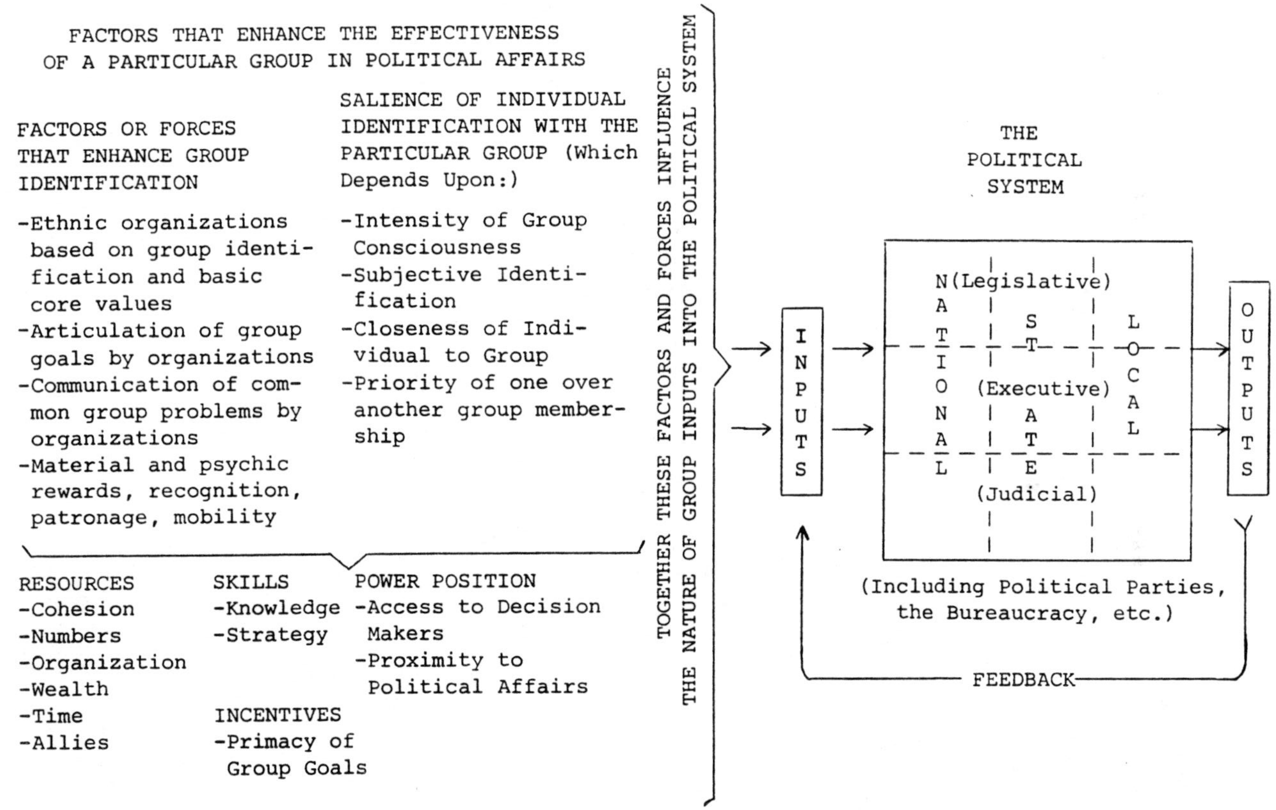

FACTORS THAT ENHANCE THE EFFECTIVENESS
OF A PARTICULAR GROUP IN POLITICAL AFFAIRS

FACTORS OR FORCES
THAT ENHANCE GROUP
IDENTIFICATION

SALIENCE OF INDIVIDUAL
IDENTIFICATION WITH THE
PARTICULAR GROUP (Which
Depends Upon:)

-Ethnic organizations
based on group identi-
fication and basic
core values

-Articulation of group
goals by organizations

-Communication of com-
mon group problems by
organizations

-Material and psychic
rewards, recognition,
patronage, mobility

-Intensity of Group
Consciousness

-Subjective Identi-
fication

-Closeness of Indi-
vidual to Group

-Priority of one over
another group member-
ship

RESOURCES
-Cohesion
-Numbers
-Organization
-Wealth
-Time
-Allies

SKILLS
-Knowledge
-Strategy

INCENTIVES
-Primacy of
Group Goals

POWER POSITION
-Access to Decision
Makers
-Proximity to
Political Affairs

THE NATURE OF GROUP INPUTS INTO THE POLITICAL SYSTEM

TOGETHER THESE FACTORS AND FORCES INFLUENCE

INPUTS

THE POLITICAL SYSTEM

NATIONAL (Legislative)
(Executive)
(Judicial)

LOCAL | STATE

OUTPUTS

(Including Political Parties,
the Bureaucracy, etc.)

FEEDBACK

15

exclusion and subordination of ethnic minority groups? Historically, Hispanics, Blacks and other ethnic groups have been victims of systematic political subordination by a dominant society which regarded them as racially and culturally inferior. Social theories such as assimilation and internal colonialism correctly characterize the discrimination, prejudice and bigotry exhibited toward these groups and the pressure brought to bear on them to embrace the culture and values of the dominant group. As the dominant society controlled all the seats of political power, it could employ any means, legal, political, or extralegal to enforce its will.

The Civil Rights Movement of the 1950's and 1960's was to minorities the second American Revolution, which changed the legal basis of political exclusion and subordination. The Civil Rights Act of 1964, the Voting Rights Acts of 1965 and 1970 and subsequent amendments, combined with several favorable Supreme Court decisions and vigorous enforcement of laws and court decrees by the Johnson and Carter administrations have swept away many of the traditional barriers to political participation by minorities. The experience of Black Americans who have been transformed into America's most powerful political ethnic group demonstrates how the fortunes of a minority can be turned around by an activist concerted effort.

Black Americans have found, however, that achieving the right to vote is not in itself the answer. It is only the first step in a broader strategy to achieve complete political integration of a minority into the political process.

Charles Hamilton has identified the central elements of a minority strategy for political change in what he calls the P Paradigm: Process, Product, Participation, where
> The process (e.g., voting, marching, caucusing, lobbying) is perceived to be related to the products sought (e.g., full employment, decent housing, good schools), participation will likely increase.(5)

In other words, according to Hamilton, achieving the right to vote does not automatically lead to the acquisition of public goods and services. The franchise is only the beginning of the harder task of transforming the vote into political power. Hamilton argues that achieving sustained participation of the

16

electorate requires that people perceive a connection between their participation and the product.

Applying all of this to the case of Hispanics, it is clear that Hispanics have not been involved in the process, due initially to political subordination by the dominant society. Many of the elements which have consolidated the black community as a viable political group are also in place among Hispanics, but need to be more effectively consolidated and mobilized to yield similar success. For example there is a plethora of Hispanic organizations which have sought to articulate what they perceive to be the central concerns and problems of Hispanics. Such groups have made a concerted effort to combine their resources by opening lines of dialogue and communication and presenting a united front before government.

The greatest task, however, remains for these groups to develop sufficient group consciousness, awareness and sensitivity to each other so that Hispanic concerns become the overriding emphasis in their collective effort to influence government and private sector corporations that could assist them.

Cross group interaction among Hispanic leaders and organizations is essential to develop the kind of cohesion that is indispensable for the development of resources, skills and incentives that will improve the Hispanic group's power position as it makes its particular claims on the political system. In recent times many of the legal barriers have been removed by the Civil Rights and Voting Rights Acts. Nonetheless, Hispanics have been slow to respond, perhaps because they have not been able to perceive the relationship between the process and the product as suggested in Hamilton's thesis. In some respects, Hispanics need to follow the path established by Blacks, but in other respects the task is more formidable. Initially the challenge to Hispanic leaders and organizations is to launch the voter registration drives that will legitimize the voting power of Hispanics. This task is complicated by the need to formalize the citizenship status of millions of Hispanics who are now classified as legal or illegal aliens. Once registered to vote, Hispanics will have to undergo a political socialization process that will make them more attuned to participatory democracy, since most Hispanics emigrated from countries with "subject" political cultures where political participation was not encouraged. Development of a strong sense of political efficacy will assure, as Hamilton recommends, a perception that process will lead to product and thus encourage further participation.

The next task for Hispanics will be to develop organizations and leadership that will serve as the basis for political coalitions representing the Hispanic community as a whole. Included will be issues that affect all Hispanics, policies and programs to address those issues, and strategies to accomplish these programs and policies.

<u>Summary</u>

In searching for an appropriate theoretical model that can accommodate ethnic minority or Hispanic politics, this chapter reviewed various political models--democratic, elite and pluralistic democracy-- along with various theoretical models offered to explain the place of minorities in American social life--internal colonialism, assimilation, melting pot and cultural pluralism. While elements of all theories were declared valid, each presented difficulties in a universal application. An eclectic approach was used to combine elements of the various theories to develop an applicable theoretical framework for the present purpose of this book. In this context Hispanics are viewed as a group which, though subordinated and excluded from politics in the past, is now capable of developing the resources and skills to more effectively compete in this pluralist society and to make claims upon the political system for benefits and advantage.

CHAPTER II

BRIEF SKETCHES: MEXICAN-AMERICANS, CUBANS,
PUERTO RICANS AND "OTHERS"

Hispanics constitute the most diverse ethnic group in American politics. No other American minority group is characterized by equal differences in race, economics, migration history, national origins and regional separation as Hispanics. Even some of the subgroups that comprise the Hispanic community are characterized by diversity. Mexican-Americans in New Mexico, for example, differ widely from their cousins in California, Arizona and Texas in their Spanish dialect, in their historical experience, in their economic and occupational status and even in self-identification. Most refer to themselves as "Spanish-American" rather than Mexican-American. Any effort to analyze the potential for a Hispanic political coalition must begin by acknowledging this diversity in origin, nationality and culture. To begin it is necessary to discuss the historical experience of each group.

The Mexican-American Experience

Two factors account for the presence of Mexican-Americans in the United States --colonization and immigration. A minority of the Mexican-American population (primarily concentrated in New Mexico and Southern Colorado with smaller numbers in Texas and California) are descended from Spanish colonists who settled in the Southwest as early as 1598.(1) By 1848 when the United States and Mexico signed the Treaty of Guadalupe Hidalgo concluding the Mexican War, there were about 75,000 persons in the area acquired by the United States, including the present states of Texas, New Mexico, Arizona, Colorado, California, Nevada and Utah.(2) Since Mexico had achieved independence from Spain in 1821 and was governing the northern territories, those people were Mexican citizens and became Mexican-Americans with the American takeover. Although it is difficult to tell exactly how many Mexican-Americans in the Southwest are descended from these colonists, it is clear that these people regard themselves as different from Mexicans who immigrated later. Some, as in New Mexico, call themselves Spanish-Americans and most regard Anglo-Americans as interlopers in their region.

By far the largest number of Mexican-Americans are immigrants or descendants of immigrants who came to the

United States after 1848. In the last century, Mexicans have continued to immigrate freely into the United States despite efforts by the United States to stop this illegal immigration. Development of irrigated farming, railroad construction and mining operations in the western states created a great demand for cheap labor in these industries. At the same time, continually depressed conditions in Mexico forced Mexican workers to look to the north for jobs and economic opportunity. These combined factors account for the millions of Mexicans who migrated to the United States since 1850. At times the U.S. allowed the immigrants entry under restricted conditions, as in the bracero program of the 1950's, but later the doors were closed and since then the U.S. has engaged in a fruitless effort to stop illegal immigration. Initially, the Mexican immigrants settled in southwestern states due to the proximity to their homeland, but recently there has been a tendency to settle in midwestern, Pacific northwestern and New England industrial centers where better jobs are available.

From the start, Mexican-Americans have struggled in the United States and the struggles have been dictated by the economic conditions they faced. Early conflict in New Mexico, Texas and California involved land. Despite U.S. guarantees promising protection of land grants, Mexican-Americans found themselves losing much of their land. Other struggles occurred in the mines, fields and factories as Mexican workers strived to secure favorable wages and working conditions. Much of this early conflict was ignored by American society, however, and the "forgotten Americans" as the Mexicans and Mexican-Americans were called, usually were victimized in land transactions and labor-management relations. As social position is dictated by employment status, Mexican-Americans lived in the poorer sections of town in conditions of poverty and deprivation. In general they contended with poorer schools and health services and were frequently targets of police brutality. They were discriminated against in education, employment and social life while suffering the humiliations of prejudice, bigotry and stereotype.

Mexican-Americans formed social, civic and political organizations both to counter the discrimination faced in society and to compensate for their exclusion from such organizations in society. Persistent efforts to partake of the political process were rebuffed by the dominant group. Only in New Mexico where Mexican-Americans were a majority of the population (until the

20

1940 census) were they able to make a significant mark in politics. Even there Mexican-Americans have had difficulty translating their political influence into economic advantage.

World War II had a significant impact on Mexican-Americans. Not only did thousands of Mexican-American men experience life outside their small towns, villages and farms, they enjoyed equal status with white Americans as soldiers. When these young men returned from the war they were unwilling to accept the discriminations and inequalities which they had experienced before the war. Mexican-Americans, moreover, had now proven their loyalty and worth as American citizens and were unwilling to accept anything less than full equality. The G.I. Bill provided untold opportunities for young Mexican-American men to attend colleges and vocational schools and to enter various professions. The war also resulted in urbanization of Mexican-Americans, traditionally a rural people but who had moved to the cities to support the American war machine. All of these factors molded the Mexican-American community into a more activist, better educated and more cohesive group. New political and social organizations emerged to steward the new political directions of the Mexican-Americans, while existing organizations like LULAC become more activist than before. The result of this new activism was the beginning of political involvement by Mexican-Americans in California, Texas, Arizona and Colorado.

In the mid-1960's, a new political wind known as the Chicano Movement enveloped the Mexican-American community, and, although most were not involved, it touched all Mexican-Americans. The term Chicano, used to refer to the Mexican-American community in the 1960's and 1970's, developed a strong political and activist connotation for the Mexican-American community. Although the movement was as philosophically diverse as the Mexican-American people themselves, the various currents somehow became melded as a singular social movement. In New Mexico, Reies Lopez Tijerina and the <u>Alianza Federal de Mercedes</u> revived the issue of the land grants. In California, Cesar Chavez advanced the first successful union to represent the cause of farm workers. In Colorado, Rodolfo "Corky" Gonzales articulated the cause of urban Chicanos. Later, Jose Angel Gutierrez launched the La Raza Unida Party in Texas. Somehow for a brief period the Mexican-American community was spiritually, if not physically, aroused by these leaders, organizations and issues. Even as the particular leaders, organizations and issues faded into the background in the 1970's and 1980's, it was clear that the Mexican-American community had experienced a new surge of ethnic consciousness and cultural pride.

Visible manifestations of the emergent Chicano identity are still seen in the determination of young Chicanos in schools and universities who continue to insist on Chicano Studies in the curriculum, while preparing themselves for professional careers where they can have a more powerful voice in the political, social and economic arena. Mexican-Americans--for the present at least--seem to have selected the path of conventional politics for political change, and, as the chapter on political participation will show, some progress has become evident.

The Puerto Rican Experience

Puerto Ricans, the second largest of the Hispanic groups, became Americans as a result of American conquests during the Spanish-American War--one remaining vestige of America's small colonial empire. The island of Puerto Rico was initially populated by the Boriquen tribe of Indians, a docile people who were taken over by the Spaniards shortly after Christopher Columbus stopped there on his second voyage and claimed the land for Spain. Those Indians who didn't die from hard labor and disease eventually mixed with Spaniards to produce the predominantly mestizo (Spanish and American Indian mixture) population of the island. Over the next four hundred years under Spanish governance, Puerto Rico became an important defensive outpost to protect Spain's new world colonial empire.(3) During that time Spain introduced black slaves from Africa to work the sugar plantations. This accounts for the black Puerto Rican population as well as for the mulattos (people of black and caucasian racial mixture).

In 1898 the United States took over the island as part of its spoils of victory in the Spanish-American War, and governed it as a colony for the next fifty years. Puerto Ricans were granted American citizenship by the Jones Act of 1917. In 1947 Puerto Rico was allowed to elect its own governor and in 1950 it was allowed to draft a constitution creating its own government.

In 1952 Puerto Rico became an American common-

22

wealth which by American standards is the closest thing to statehood. Puerto Ricans have in fact debated the relative merits of statehood and independence over their present status and have seemed to prefer their commonwealth status. Under this arrangement Puerto Ricans as American citizens are assured of a common defense and common trade (free trade between the island and mainland) and a common currency. Although independence would give Puerto Rico greater control of its own affairs and its economy--especially considering newly discovered oil deposits--it would also mean an end to extensive U.S. government economic aid, welfare subsidies and other federal aid. Statehood would assure Puerto Ricans of a stronger voice in American political affairs, but it would also limit the control they now have over their own affairs.

Because Puerto Rico's 3,380,000 residents are American citizens, they can migrate to and from the mainland at will. There are presently 1,800,000 Puerto Ricans in the mainland U.S. Since Puerto Ricans are primarily Spanish-speaking mestizos, their adjustment in the United States has not been easy. They have frequently experienced some of the same discrimination and prejudice faced by Blacks and their Mexican cousins in the United States. Puerto Ricans have also been characterized by poverty, low levels of education and limited formal training for employment; thus they have faced economic hardship both on the island and as immigrants to the mainland.

The greatest concentration of Puerto Ricans has been in New York where over a million now reside. Although they constitute 10 percent of the population in New York City, their influence is limited because only 30 percent are registered to vote. Puerto Ricans have elected two congressmen and several city council members, but their overall representation in New York's vast bureaucracy is very small. Although the social demographic factors of the Puerto Rican population are not encouraging, Puerto Ricans do constitute a potentially important political group, especially when considering their concentration in cities and the possibility of a larger Hispanic coalition.

The Cuban-American Experience

Cuban-American immigration to the United States differs from that of other Hispanic groups in various respects. First, it is more recent. Second, it stems primarily from political rather than economic causes.

23

Fidel Castro's successful revolution against the Cuban dictatorship of Fulgencio Batista in 1959 leading to Cuba's present status as a Communist state acted as a powerful impetus for Cuban immigration to the United States.

The island of Cuba was discovered by Christopher Columbus on his first voyage to the new world in 1492. He described it as "the most beautiful land that my eyes had ever seen."(4) The Spaniards established several settlements, and over the next half century most of the original Indian settlers, the Arawak Indians, were killed either in warfare or by disease. (The Spaniards introduced smallpox which decimated the Indian population.) Some who survived were integrated into Spanish society, and account for Cuba's mestizos. Beginning in 1822 Spain imported black slaves to provide an agricultural labor force and this accounts for Cuba's black and mulatto population. Through the 17th and 18th centuries Cuba was prey to attacks by pirates and Spain's rivals in the new world. In the mid-19th century several efforts at Cuban independence failed. In 1895 a new independence effort was initiated by Jose Julian Marti who was killed, becoming Cuba's national hero. The war continued and in 1898 the U.S.S. Maine exploded in Havana Harbor, plunging the U.S. into war with Spain. The Treaty of Paris of 1898 ended the Spanish-American War and forced Spain to relinquish Cuba which was then occupied by the United States. In 1901 a constitution was adopted with the Platt Amendment which allowed the U.S. to intervene in the island's internal affairs. Cuba was riddled by instability for the next fifty years, with frequent changes in government. In 1952 Fulgencio Batista seized power in a bloodless coup. Elected President in 1954, he ruled essentially as a dictator.

Batista himself was overthrown on January 1, 1959 by a revolution led by Fidel Castro. Castro established an authoritarian Communist state, nationalizing business, expropriating foreign properties and taking over the economy. The U.S. broke diplomatic relations in 1961 and in 1962 supported the ill-fated Bay of Pigs invasion carried out by Cuban refugees. The U.S. imposed an economic blockade of Cuba which forced Castro into greater dependence on the Soviet Union. United States-Cuban relations reached a nadir during the Cuban Missile Crisis of October, 1962 when the U.S. discovered construction of offensive missile bases in Cuba. The bases were eventually dismantled, but not before bringing the two world powers to the brink of nuclear war. Since that time Cuba has been a Soviet bloc communist nation and an acknowledged American adversary, supporting revolutionary movements in various Latin American countries.

In 1965 Castro allowed willing Cubans to leave the country, and hundreds of thousands of Cubans left, primarily to the United States. The contrast between these early Cuban refugees and other Hispanic immigrants is important. Since most were of the well-educated middle class, they adapted readily to their new environment. Beginning as service workers and taxi drivers these Cuban-Americans quickly progressed and many now own their own businesses or have become professionals.

In 1980 President Carter allowed 150,000 Cubans to enter Florida through the Mariel Boatlift. This latest wave of Cuban refugees brought mostly lower class and unskilled people. Castro used the exodus to empty Cuban prisons of convicts, the mentally retarded and other undesirables. Many of these immigrants were detained in refugee camps for months before being processed for relocation or return to Cuba.

Because of its proximity to Cuba in distance and climate, Florida has attracted the bulk of Cubans; the population of Miami alone includes over 580,000 Cubans. Other Cubans have settled primarily in New York City. Initially, Cubans were reluctant to establish roots and become naturalized citizens because they hoped that Castro would not survive and they could return home. However, many have now begun the process of integrating into American culture. Cubans who settled in Florida, especially Miami, have been very successful in integrating into American economic and political life because of their education and industry, and will surely become a greater force in Dade County and Florida politics in the years to come.

Other Hispanics

More diverse than the other clearly identifiable Hispanic groups are the people labelled here as "Other Hispanics." These people include every identifiable nationality of people who came from Spain or any other country ever under Spain's influence. This includes, of course, all of the Latin American countries (except Brazil which was colonized by Portugal) that have been at one time or another major sources of immigration to the United States.

The imperfect method of self-identification used by the U.S. Census Bureau in identifying Hispanics means that many in the category labelled "Other Hispanics" are actually Mexican-Americans, Puerto Ricans or Cubans, so it is important to note that the 3 million people thus identified may belong to one of the three main groups.

There are, however, large numbers of Hispanics who have immigrated from Spain or Latin American countries. It is noteworthy that immigration to the U.S. from other western hemispheric countries was encouraged by limited restrictions. Even early quota limits on immigration applied to other nations did not apply to western hemisphere countries. Only in immigration laws passed in the 1960's have restrictions been applied.

The latest waves of Latin American immigration are undoubtedly from civil war-torn Central American countries such as El Salvador and Nicaragua. Many of these people have been allowed entry as political refugees while others have entered illegally. The true number of these people entering the United States is not known, however, because many of them migrate north to Mexico and cross the border along with many illegal Mexican aliens.

One important political note about the people labelled "Other Hispanic" is that because their numbers are smaller than the three main groups, they are likely to be forgotten as a subgroup unless they are embraced by the broader concept of Hispanics with which they can be identified.

Patterns of Accommodation of Hispanics in the U.S.

Considering the diverse migration history of the various Hispanic groups to the United States, it is not surprising that there are differences in their level of acculturation and integration in this country. Two of the subgroups, Mexicans and Cubans, tend to feel more "separated" from their home countries and are more accommodated to their status as permanent residents. Puerto Ricans and "Other Hispanics," on the other hand, appear to prefer the "visitor" status. Mexican and Cuban-Americans are more likely to own their own homes and are less likely to indicate a desire to visit their home country or to relocate there if economic and political situations changed.(5) Mexicans are the most assimilated of Hispanic groups with the highest proportion (53 percent) born in the United States and the highest level of bi-lingualism (60 percent). Their $16,300 average annual household income reflects that their status is better than other Hispanic groups (other than Cubans), though by American standards, they are still in the category of economically disadvantaged. Despite their high level of assimilation, Mexicans regard their Hispanic identity as equally important to their status as Americans.(6)

Cubans are an older, well-educated, "almost aristocratic" group of people. Many Cuban-Americans were professionals, the upper class of Cuban society, who became refugees when Castro took power. Cubans thus have the highest average annual household income ($21,300) of any Hispanic group and the highest rate of mobility, 38 percent being white collar workers. More Cubans (about 74 percent) regard themselves as Hispanic first and Americans second, and are more likely to speak Spanish than be bilingual. These characteristics are probably due to their more recent arrival in the United States. Because of their higher educational level and more aggressive character it is likely that they will readily adapt to the new language and competitive American life-style once they become resigned to remain in the United States. Of course, the more recent Cuban emigres who arrive during the Mariel Boatlift include poorer, less educated Cubans who more closely resemble other Hispanic immigrants.(7)

Because Puerto Ricans have greater freedom to migrate between the mainland and Puerto Rico, fewer of this group are committed to a permanent status in the U.S. Only 18 percent were born in the U.S. and most (60 percent) are bilingual. The majority indicate their intent to return to Puerto Rico to live permanently. Puerto Ricans are the least educated and have the lowest average annual household income ($11,400) of all Hispanic groups, often working in unskilled occupations.

The "Other Hispanics" are the most recent immigrants, most having arrived within the past ten years. Many in this group are young and single and only about 40 percent speak English. They compensate, however, by being better educated and trained than other immigrants. Many of this group view themselves as refugees from political repression and violence in their home countries and regard the United States as a temporary safe haven until the political situation changes at home and they can return.(8)

A Socioeconomic Profile of Hispanics

Although Hispanics have made some progress, their overall socioeconomic status remains considerably below that of the white American population. Even here there is some deviation between Hispanic groups as Cubans fare better than others. Overall, however, parallels in economic disadvantage afflict all Hispanics and could serve as the unifying characteristic needed for greater group cohesion. The median income of Hispanics in 1981 was $16,227 which was 70 percent of the median income of the whites at $23,907. Cubans had the highest median income of Hispanic groups with $17,538 followed by Mexican-Americans and "Other Hispanics" with $15,171. The Puerto Rican median income of $9,855 was barely above the 1981 recognized poverty level of $9,287. The Census Bureau estimated that there were 800,000 Hispanic families living below the poverty level in 1981. Thus almost one-fourth of all Hispanic families fell below the poverty level as compared to 8.8 percent of white families.(9)

Employment

As employment dictates economic status, Hispanics are still found predominantly in lower status and lower paid occupations, although they do show some improvement from previous years. Although Hispanic men showed a higher level of participation (85.2 percent) in the workforce than all adult men (79.4 percent), their income was lower due to their higher presence in unskilled, service and operative (a type of laboring) occupations. Of Hispanic women, 48.8 percent are in the workforce, slightly lower than the figure of 51.3 percent for all women. Again, their wages are generally lower due to their concentration in unskilled, service-type work. Underemployment continues to be a chronic problem for both Hispanic men and women, although there has been some progress. The number of Hispanic men employed in professional, technical and managerial jobs rose from 32 percent in 1973 to 36 percent in 1982. Also, the number of Hispanic women in clerical jobs rose from 41 percent in 1973 to 49 percent in 1982. Cuban-Americans are more likely than other Hispanics to hold professional, technical or managerial jobs. Data indicate that 27 percent of Cubans hold professional, technical or managerial jobs as compared to 15.4 percent for Puerto Ricans and 12 percent for Mexican-Americans.(10)

Unemployment among Hispanics runs as high as 50

percent, with Puerto Ricans exhibiting the highest rate and Cubans the lowest.(11)

Education

Increased education invariably accounts for improved job opportunities. Consequently, the degree of progress achieved by Hispanics in education fore-tells whether the employment picture will improve. While only 33.4 percent of Hispanic males and 31 percent of Hispanic females completed high school in 1970, the numbers increased to 45.5 for males and 43.6 for females by 1981. However, this was still much lower than the 70.3 percent for white males and 69.1 for white females. Although Hispanic college enroll-ment doubled from one-quarter million to one-half million between 1972 and 1981, Hispanics accounted for only 4.8 percent of the total college enrollment in 1981. Moreover, less than half (43 percent of males and 46 percent of females) of the Hispanics who en-rolled in college received their degrees as compared to 76 percent for non-Hispanics.(12)   Again, Cuban-Amer-icans are the most likely to have completed high school and college.

Family Status

The family, traditionally the anchor of Hispanic culture, has declined as an institution among Hispanics in American life. Seventy three percent of Hispanics live in family groups compared to 81.7 percent for non-Hispanics. The number of single parent families, usually headed by a female, is greater (23 percent) than for non-Hispanics (15 percent).(13)

Although educational, employment and economic indicators show improvement among Hispanics during the past ten years, the overall socioeconomic condition of Hispanics is still very marginal as compared to the American population as a whole. American government's response to the economic disadvantage of its Hispanic population has been limited due to the lack of politi-cal clout which the group has had in Washington. This situation will have to change if Hispanics are to achieve further economic improvement.

Summary

This chapter has described the diversity of Hispanic Americans by outlining the specific historical and political background of each group and the circumstances that led to their becoming American. The chapter also highlighted the dismal socioeconomic picture of Hispanics and their perception of their status in American life. Although some Mexican-Americans owe their origins to pre-American Spanish colonization of the Southwest, most of this group immigrated to the United States in search of economic opportunity. Puerto Ricans became Americans as a result of their territorial status following the Spanish-American War. Cuban migration to the United States was motivated by a desire to escape political repression in Cuba. Other Hispanic-Americans, especially refugees from Central American countries, have continued to migrate in recent years to escape political violence and unrest in their countries. Although all groups have displayed a willingness to embrace American society and culture, all have insisted on retaining their Hispanic identity and language. Cuban-Americans have enjoyed greater economic success because of their education and professional preparation, while other groups have experienced greater deprivation due to lower levels of education and their unskilled status. Still, the overall economic condition of Hispanics in American life is dismal and governmental responses have been limited due to the limited political clout of the group.

CHAPTER III

THE HISPANIC VOTE

Unlike the Black vote which has exhibited remarkable cohesion, supporting the Democratic Party in the last three Presidential elections, the Hispanic vote has yet to show such cohesion and support for one party. Ronald Reagan won the last two Presidential elections even though he lost the Hispanic vote; but even if the Democrats had won, Hispanic claims upon the Democrats would have been diminished by the less than overwhelming support given that party by Hispanics.

Conditions and Importance of the Hispanic Vote

The significance of Hispanic voting in Presidential elections will determine whether Hispanics can become, like Blacks, a pivotal vote in a close election and will also determine the claims Hispanics can make on the winning party as a reward for the group's support. Because Hispanic support has benefitted the Democratic Party, it is assumed that they will receive more favored treatment from the Democrats and will generally agonize during periods of Republican hegemony. Hispanic voting in Presidential elections is tied to such external forces as national and international events, economic conditions, the influence of mass media and political organization. It is also influenced by internal factors such as political values, voter awareness, political leadership and political awareness and participation. All of these factors constitute the political environment under which Hispanics will vote. Under normal conditions Hispanics tend to favor the Democrats, but alterations in the norms could yield a reversal in the historical pattern or could affect the margin of Hispanic support the Democrats receive.

This section will examine Hispanic voting in national and state elections. It will attempt to uncover trends in Hispanic voter preference and offer explanations for those trends. It will explore the possibilities for and obstacles to a more cohesive and viable Hispanic vote. The Hispanic vote in a Presidential election assumes importance not only as a barometer of Hispanic political participation and as a symbolic expression of Hispanic values and preferences, but from a national perspective serves as a measure of power the group wields in determining the outcome of an election and in making claims upon government.

Although completely reliable public opinion polls measuring Hispanic voter preferences in national elections are not yet available, a preliminary picture of Hispanic voter preferences has begun to appear in the national polls conducted by the major polling organizations, Gallup and Roper and in the exit polls conducted by the major television networks following Presidential elections. In 1984 all three television networks conducted exit polls as part of their General Election coverage, and all attempted to identify distinct voter preferences among ethnic groups on a national level. Some of the polls, however, failed to include Hispanic samples in key representative states; thus their utility for the present analysis is limited. NBC, for example, omitted Hispanic samples in New York and New Jersey while CBS included only New York, California and Texas (excluding Florida and New Jersey), thus limiting their overall national application and regional comparisons.

The ABC News Poll

Because the poll conducted by ABC News comes closest to including all of the key Hispanic regions, the following analysis will rely on that data. ABC News interviewed a total of 11,023 voters in their exit poll following the 1984 General Election; about 3 percent (or about 331) were Hispanics.(1)

Table III offers a comparison of the 1980 and 1984 voter preferences of White, Hispanic and Black voters. Although Hispanics gave their support to the Democratic Party candidates, Carter in 1980 and Mondale in 1984, the margin was less than overwhelming when compared to the Black vote. The 82 percent Carter received in 1980 and the 89 percent Mondale received in 1984 clearly indicate that although the Black community is itself a coalition of diverse localized and specialized subgroups, it shows remarkable collective expression as "the Black vote" in national elections. Such is not the case with Hispanics.

Hispanics gave the incumbent Jimmy Carter only a slight majority of 55 percent in the 1980 Presidential election; 37 percent voted for Reagan and 7 percent voted for Independent candidate John Anderson. Carter's relatively "poor" showing among Hispanics suggests that his numerous appointments of Hispanics (see Chapter 4) failed to assure him of widespread support within that group. In the 1984 election Mondale received only 56 percent of the Hispanic vote, notwith-

TABLE III

COMPARISON OF 1980 AND 1984 ABC EXIT POLL RESULTS:

WHITE, HISPANIC AND BLACK VOTERS

CANDIDATE/ YEAR	WHITES %	HISPANICS %	BLACKS %
1980			
Reagan (R)	55	37	13
Carter (D)	34	55	82
Anderson (I)	9	7	4
1984			
Reagan (R)	63	44	11
Mondale (D)	37	56	89

Source: ABC News Polling Unit, "ABC News Poll--Year-End Wrapup,"
1985.

standing President Reagan's lackluster performance on social and economic issues of concern to Hispanics and his failure to appoint many Hispanics to high govern-positions.

Table IV, which summarizes the 1984 ABC News Exit Poll results of Hispanic and White presidential voting, suggests where some of the fractionalization of the Hispanic vote occurred. Nationally, Mondale received 56 percent of the Hispanic vote to Reagan's 44 percent. This was a complete reversal of the margins which White voters were giving Reagan and which accounted for his landslide victory. Hispanics gave Mondale majority support in all but four of the twelve states polled by ABC News. The 73 percent of the vote given Reagan by Hispanic voters in Florida reinforces the assumption that Cuban voters deviate from other normal Hispanic support of liberal Democratic Party candidates. The Reagan margins in Mississippi and North Carolina suggest, perhaps, that Cuban concentrations in other southern states (like Florida) may be reflective of a wider Hispanic southern block of voters who prefer the Republican Party and conservative candidates. The Reagan margin of Hispanic support in New Jersey is harder to explain, considering that the predominant Hispanic group in that state has been Puerto Rican. Apparently the Cuban influence in New Jersey is increasing to the extent that it neutralizes the pro-Democrat Puerto Rican vote. In New York the 60 percent received by Mondale reflects the traditional Puerto Rican preference for the Democratic Party, but the forty percent received by Reagan must be disturbing to Democratic candidates. Again, Cuban influence may be increasing in New York to the extent that it is neutralizing the normal Puerto Rican support of Democrats. Elsewhere in the country where Mexican-Americans are the predominant Hispanic group, Mondale and the Democrats received majorities (varying in size from 57 percent in California to 76 percent in Texas) even as Reagan was winning the election in each state.

In their partisan preference, Hispanics, like Blacks, established strong association with the Democratic Party following the Great Depression of the 1930's and the subsequent Roosevelt revolution. However, as indicated above, their affinity to the Democrats has not been as overwhelming as has been with the Blacks. Hispanics--at least counted as a group--seem to resemble other ethnic groups with only moderate preference for the Democrats. Jews and Italians, for example, gave majority support to the Democratic Party:

TABLE IV

1984 ABC NEWS EXIT POLL--HISPANIC AND WHITE VOTE FOR PRESIDENT

	POLL	% VOTERS	MONDALE	REAGAN	OTHER
NATIONAL	HISPANIC	3	56	44	0
(11,023)a	WHITE	88	37	63	0
CALIFORNIA	HISPANIC	10	57	42	1
(1,163)a	WHITE	84	39	60	1
FLORIDA	HISPANIC	3	27	73	0
(991)a	WHITE	91	29	71	0
ILLINOIS	HISPANIC	1	82	18	0
(972)a	WHITE	86	37	63	0
IOWA	HISPANIC	1	86	14	0
(1,213)a	WHITE	95	52	58	0
MASSACHUSETTS	HISPANIC	1	78	22	0
(1,096)a	WHITE	94	50	49	1
MICHIGAN	HISPANIC	1	67	33	0
(1,043)a	WHITE	87	37	62	1
MISSISSIPPI	HISPANIC	1	40	60	0
(782)a	WHITE	74	15	85	0
NEW JERSEY	HISPANIC	2	35	65	0
(1,244)a	WHITE	93	37	63	0
NEW YORK	HISPANIC	6	60	40	0
(1,454)a	WHITE	84	44	56	0
NORTH CAROLINA	HISPANIC	1	17	83	0
(1,205)a	WHITE	86	29	71	0
OHIO	HISPANIC	1	57	43	0
(1,081)a	WHITE	87	34	66	0
TEXAS	HISPANIC	7	76	24	0
(1,076)a	WHITE	88	27	73	0

a   Total number of interviews.

Source: ABC News Polling Unit, "ABC News Poll, Year-End Wrapup,"
1985.

that support, however, was less than overwhelming be-
because of pockets of voters who for various reasons
favored the Republican Party. The Cuban preference for
the Republican Party thus resembles the "confident and
prosperous" Northern Italians who preferred the Republican Party.(2)

NBC News 1984 Exit Poll

The NBC News 1984 General Election day exit poll
results generally affirm the conclusions drawn from the
ABC poll, although the percentages and margins differ
because different states were polled. NBC interviewed
a total of 11,671 voters in 400 locations throughout
the country.(3) Although the percentage of those
polled who were Hispanic is not provided, the data
obtained from those states and voting districts where
NBC polled Hispanics enabled them to offer conclusions
on the Hispanic vote in 1984. NBC News polling showed
that the Democrat Mondale received 68 percent of the
Hispanic vote to 32 percent for Reagan/Bush in the
three states where Hispanic voters were polled (California, Texas and Florida). In California, Hispanics
gave Mondale 76 percent to Reagan's 24 percent, while
the incumbent President received 64 percent of the
White vote. In Texas, Mondale received 65 percent of
the Hispanic vote to Reagan's 35 percent, while White
voters were giving Reagan 74 percent of the vote. In
Florida, Hispanic voters of predominantly Cuban origin
resulted in a 68 percent majority for Reagan among
Hispanics as compared to the 72 percent Reagan received
from White voters.

NBC polling also disclosed strong Hispanic voter
preference for Democratic Party candidates for Congress, as 71 percent of Hispanic voters said they had
voted for Democrats and 26 percent voted for Republicans. Two percent didn't vote and one percent voted
for "Others."

The strong support Hispanics (with the exception
of Cubans) lent the Democratic candidates in the 1980
and 1984 elections suggests the possibility of an
Hispanic-Black ethnic coalition. Mexican-Americans and
Puerto Rican support for the Democrats seems consistent, if not overwhelming, and when combined with the
overwhelming preference Blacks accord the Democrats,
could produce an ethnic coalition which could be
pivotal in a Presidential contest, especially a close
one. Such a coalition is plausible not only because of
the similarity in the socioeconomic conditions of both

groups and their traditional status as subordinated minorities, but because of initiatives by Black and Hispanic leaders such as New Mexico Governor Toney Anaya and Chicago Mayor Harold Washington to work together for such coalitions (see Chapter 5).

Partisanship, Age, Philosophical and Issue Orientations of Hispanic Voters

Besides reaffirming some of the previous election-day preferences of Hispanic voters uncovered by the other networks, The CBS /New York Times election day exit polls provided important new insights on the age, sex, partisanship, philosophical and issue orientations of Hispanic voters. Their study was limited to New York, California and Texas, so we can discern that those conclusions apply mainly to Puerto Ricans in New York and Mexican-Americans in California and Texas. Table V summarizes the age, sex and partisanship of Hispanic voters polled in the CBS 1984 General Election exit poll. The 66 Hispanic voters polled in New York constituted 3 percent of the sample, while 64 were polled in California (6 percent of the sample) and 142 in Texas (7 percent of the sample). The table shows that in New York and Texas, female Hispanics outnumbered male Hispanic voters by 18 to 10 percentage points respectively, while in California male voters outnumbered women by 10 percentage points. No explanation is offered for these results.

The relative youth of Hispanic voters is reflected in the table which shows the 18-29 group being the most numerous in New York (41 percent) and Texas (36 percent) and the second largest in California (32 percent). The table shows that in almost all cases the majority of Hispanic voters fall in the two youngest categories of voters (ages 18-44), with "others" being the most numerous in the older categories (ages 45 or older). Those figures affirm that the younger age of the Hispanic voters could prove to be an asset in the long run.

As expected, the majority of Hispanics identify as Democrats in all three states, with the number of Republicans being highest in New York. In all cases the majority of Hispanics label themselves as Democrats even though the party balance is much closer among the remaining non-Hispanic population. This indicates that Hispanics (at least the Mexican-Americans and Puerto Ricans) perceive themselves as tied to the Democratic Party regardless of their vote in a particular

37

TABLE V

AGE, SEX, PARTISANSHIP AND PHILOSOPHICAL ORIENTATIONS

OF HISPANIC VOTERS--NEW YORK, CALIFORNIA, AND TEXAS, 1984

| | NEW YORK | | CALIFORNIA | | TEXAS | |
	HISPANIC	OTHER	HISPANIC	OTHER	HISPANIC	OTHER
N = (weighted)	66	2,181	164	2,571	142	1,833
SEX						
MALE	41%	48%	55%	47%	45%	51%
FEMALE	59	52	45	53	55	49
AGE						
18-29	41	25	32	22	36	27
30-44	29	32	40	29	33	36
45-59	15	22	19	23	24	21
60 +	15	20	9	25	7	16
PARTY ID						
REPUBLICAN	29	33	22	42	19	34
DEMOCRAT	58	41	64	39	59	38
INDEPENDENT	13	24	13	17	21	26
POLITICAL PHILOSOPHY						
LIBERAL	31	24	25	19	24	14
MODERATE	33	39	35	43	44	38
CONSERVATIVE	30	33	34	34	28	44

Source: CBS News/New York Times Polls, National Election Day,
1984. "Hispanics vs. Other Voters."

election.

In self-proclaimed political philosophy, Hispanics in New York divide about equally into thirds in identifying themselves as liberals, moderates and conservatives. In California, only a fourth identify themselves as liberal; almost equal numbers identify themselves as moderates (35 percent) or conservatives (34 percent). In Texas, 44 percent proclaim moderate philosophy and one quarter each fall into the liberal and conservative camps. These pronouncements may come as a surprise to observers who have perceived Hispanics as "liberals." The figures instead suggest fairly high numbers of conservatives and moderates among Hispanic voters.

With respect to issue orientations, Hispanics expressed greatest concern over "arms control" with 38 percent of Hispanic voters selecting it as the most important of eight issues in influencing their vote in the 1984 Presidential election. The "economy" was identified as the second most important issue to Hispanics with 29 percent identifying it as influencing their vote. By way of comparison, White Americans (41 percent) listed the economy as most important, with arms control and "strong defense" tied for second at 28 percent. Black Americans rated "fairness to poor" as the prime issue (51 percent) and the economy (31 percent) second. "Fairness to poor" ranked third (28 percent) in importance among Hispanics. Although Hispanics are generally poor, poverty issues are apparently not paramount in influencing Hispanic voting decisions, even though they are concerned about economic issues which may limit job opportunities. Fifty-one percent of Hispanics favored an increase in federal spending for the poor compared to 72 percent for Blacks. Thirty-one percent of Hispanics felt present spending levels for the poor are adequate (compared to 16 percent for Blacks) and 8 percent favored reductions.

Interestingly, Hispanics did not rank "Central America" (8 percent) nor "abortion" (7 percent) as particularly important issues in influencing their voting decision even though Central America affects fellow Hispanics and abortion is an issue of particular importance to Catholics, the predominant Hispanic religion. Responding to a question on whether abortion should be legalized, only 27 percent expressed a categoric no, 33 percent supported abortion in extreme cases and 38 percent favored abortion on demand. Their disapproval of legalized abortion differed only marginally from the position of Blacks and Whites on the issue. Questioned whether the Communist threat in Central America warranted American troop presence in the region, 47 percent of Hispanics agreed while 53 percent of Whites supported troop presence in Central America. The 49 percent of Hispanics who disagreed with the need for troops in Central America suggests that Hispanics are sharply divided between those who favor self-determination for Central Americans without U.S. involvement and those who favor an active U.S. presence in the region.

On the issue of "negotiating a nuclear freeze," Hispanic support (52 percent) was lower than that of Blacks (57 percent) and slightly higher than White support (46 percent).

In response to questions regarding reasons for their choice for President, Hispanics rated the "economy" first, "arms control" second and "federal budget deficit" third. Forty percent of Hispanics contended that their choice of Presidential candidate was based on "his vision for the future" and "strong leadership" was rated second.(4)

All of these responses indicate that Hispanics express liberal to moderate orientations on most issues but their support for those issues is not as intense as among Blacks. Hispanics, although concerned about the "economy" and how it might affect job opportunities, do not generally advocate increased government spending for the poor as much as Blacks do. Hispanics also do not differ markedly from other groups on those issues such as Central America and abortion which would seem to be of special concern to Hispanics. Finally, Hispanics seem more concerned about the need for "arms control" and "negotiations for a nuclear freeze" than other groups.

The Hispanic Vote in State and Local Elections

While the Hispanic vote has been inconclusive in national politics it has in several instances demonstrated the necessary cohesion and ability to influence election outcomes at the state and local level. New Mexico's Mexican-American voters have been an active, informed and highly participant electorate since attaining statehood.(5) Texas' Mexican-American voters have figured prominently in the politics of specific regions. In San Antonio, they figured prominently in the elections of Congressman Henry B. Gonzales since 1961 and more recently the election of San Antonio Mayor Henry Cisneros and Congressman Albert Bustamante.(6) In the south Texas region, Mexican-Americans have supported E. "Kika" de la Garza since 1964, and recently elected another Hispanic Congressman, Solomon Ortiz. Ortiz has long been a popular Nueces County (Corpus Christi) politician who has received solid support from Hispanics. In Brownsville, which is now part of Ortiz' district, Hispanic voters elected Emilio Hernandez as Mayor. In the Los Angeles, California area, Mexican-American voters have figured prominently in the victories of Congressman Edward Roybal since 1962 and most recently have helped elect Congressmen Matthew "Marty" Martinez and Esteban Torres and City Councillor Richard Alatorre. In Colorado, Mexican-American voters in Denver helped elect that city's first Hispanic Mayor, Federico Pena, and have also elected several state legislators.

Puerto Ricans in the South Bronx in New York City have similarly given support to their own candidates for Congress, initially Herman Badillo in the 1960's and more recently Robert Garcia. They have also elected several city councilors.

In Florida, Hispanics helped elect Maurice Ferre and Xavier Suarez as Mayors of Miami, Robert Martinez as Mayor of Tampa and Raul Martinez as Mayor of Hialeah.

There are many other instances throughout the country where Hispanic voter participation, as described above, has contributed to elections of Hispanic politicians to state legislative, county, municipal and school board positions. These are, however, too numerous to describe here. Instead, specific examples of Hispanic voting as it contributed to Hispanic electoral victories are provided in Chapters 4 and 5. These examples of Hispanic participation do not negate the general assumption that Hispanic voter participation is below that of the general population and other minority groups such as Blacks.

According to a report by the U.S. Census Bureau, only about 36 percent of Hispanics of voting age were registered to vote in 1980. This compares with 69 percent for non-Hispanics. The figures are lower for actual voting, as only 30 percent of Hispanics of voting age actually voted in 1980 compared to 61 percent for non-Hispanics. According to the Census Bureau, only 46 percent of Hispanics between 18 and 34 are registered to vote. Since that age group makes up 58 percent of the Hispanic population in the United States, the loss of voting power is as great as is its potential influence if it were mobilized. Among Hispanic voters Cubans, perhaps because of higher education and socioeconomic levels, have the highest levels of voter registration with 75 percent registering to vote. In comparison, 58 percent of Mexican-Americans and 55 percent of Puerto Ricans were registered to vote in 1980.(7)

Indications are that voter registration and actual voting rates have gone up in recent years, perhaps because of voter registration drives launched by groups such as the Southwest Voter Registration and Education Project (SWVREP) among Mexican-Americans and the National Puerto Rican/Hispanic Voter Participation Project among Puerto Ricans.(8) In 1976 only 32 percent of Hispanics voted but this increased to 44 percent in the 1980 Presidential election. Results for the 1984 Presidential election will probably demonstrate a further increase as a result of the aforementioned voter registration efforts.

Factors Contributing to Hispanic Political Participation

In view of the comparatively low levels of political participation among Hispanics and the need to reverse the trend if Hispanics are to improve their political position in American politics, it is appropriate to consider possible factors which have contributed to low participation and what can be done to address them. Rodolfo de la Garza and Robert Brischetto have attempted to answer some of those questions, at least as they apply to Mexican-Americans in the Southwest. One study explored five dimensions of Mexican-American political participation including registration, voting and other forms of electioneering in East Los Angeles and San Antonio.(9) The authors found fairly high levels of registration, 76 percent among Hispanics in San Antonio and 67 percent in East Los Angeles in their sample, suggesting that, as indicated before, the registration of Hispanics in selected areas is fairly close to general population levels, even if overall Hispanic population figures are lower. In actual voting in the 1980 election, however, Hispanic participation declined to 60 percent in San Antonio and 55 percent in East Los Angeles (and declined even furfurther to about 30 percent in "electioneering").(10)

In considering some factors that may result in lower levels of participation among Hispanics, the authors focused on some familiar explanations which have been cited in previous studies on non-voting. These include political alienation, age, education, gender, occupation and income which either alone or in combination have discouraged Hispanic voting. The authors found about normal levels of interest among their respondents with 32 percent "very interested," 39 percent "somewhat interested," and 29 percent "not very interested" in politics.

Political alienation from the American political system, which has sometimes been offered as a cause for non-participation by minorities, was not inordinately high for Hispanics in either city, with about 32 percent expressing the view that "people don't have any say" in politics. A relatively high proportion of respondents, 47 percent, expressed the view that "public officials don't care," suggesting that Hispanics may feel that the political system is not very interested in or responsive to their particular problems. A very high proportion, 70 percent, indicated that "politics is too complicated," suggesting that rather than being alienated from politics, Hispanics may find American politics too difficult and confusing.(11)

Hispanics report slightly lower levels of interest in politics than the general population, according to the authors, but generally reflect the same trends among respective age groups. Middle-aged Hispanic voters (45 to 65) are most likely to show high levels of interest in politics. Younger voters (18-35) are "somewhat interested" and oldest voters (above 65) are "not very interested in politics."(12)

Relative to marriage and gender, Brischetto and de la Garza found that married Hispanics were more likely to register and vote than single persons, although Hispanic women who were single show a greater inclination to register and vote than single Hispanic males.(13)

Educational attainment has the same effect on Hispanic political participation as on the general population, with levels of participation increasing in proportion to the level of education achieved. For example, in 1980, 69 percent of Hispanics with 8 years or less of education registered and 57 percent voted as compared to the 81 percent registered and 66 percent who voted among Hispanics who had some college. The same trends were found relative to employment and occupational status. Employed Hispanics showed much higher levels of registration (77 percent) and voting (63 percent) than those who were unemployed (52 and 35 percent respectively). Those Hispanics employed in the professional, technical and managerial fields showed much higher levels of registration (87 percent) and voting (74 percent) than those in laboring and service type occupations (67 percent and 52 percent, respectively.)(14)

Although the pattern of political passivity among Mexican-American voters reported by Brischetto and de la Garza is generally similar to the general population relative to age, education, gender, employment and occupation, its impact seems to be greater on Hispanic non-participation. Confusion and ignorance about American politics, lower levels of education, concentration in lower paying occupations and their younger age appear to be quite significant factors in accounting for the lower levels of interest in politics, registration, voting and other forms of political participation among Hispanics.

One other factor which could contribute to Hispanic non-participation is the phenomenon of fear. Although this writer does not know of any scholarly effort to gauge whether "fear of voting" has been a factor in non-participation among Hispanics, the phenomenon has been found to be a factor among similar minority populations, notably Black Americans. At least one study by Douglas St. Angelo and Paul Puryear(15) suggested that fear was a more important cause of Black non-voting than levels of education, income and occupation. Because of the comparatively similar social circumstances of Hispanics and Blacks, it is possible that "fear of voting" could be a further contributing factor to Hispanic non-participation.

Summary

This chapter has shown that while Hispanics have the potential for being a pivotal vote in national elections, they have yet to reach their peak due to comparatively low levels of participation and lack of cohesion. The Hispanic vote still needs to be mobilized if it is to become a force in national politics. Still, the concentration of Hispanics in the large states and their general support for the Democratic Party even in a losing year (1984) suggests the potential for a bloc vote. Hispanics, however, are not as cohesive as Blacks due partly to internal fractionalization such as the tendency of Cubans to support Republican candidates as they did Ronald Reagan in 1984. Analysis of ABC and NBC exit polling in the 1984 Presidential election showed strong but not over-whelming support for Democrat Walter Mondale among Mexican-American and Puerto Rican voters, but equally strong support for Reagan by Cubans.

Analysis of CBS News exit polls confirm that the bulk of Hispanic voters are in the young (18-44) age group, and aside from Cubans, identify with the Democratic Party. Philosophically, most Hispanics tend to identify themselves as "moderates" with one-third labeling themselves as "liberals" and one fourth as "conservatives." This dispels the traditional assumption of Hispanics as "liberals."

Relative to issue orientations, Hispanics express greatest concern over "arms control" and the "economy." Their high ranking of economic issues but comparatively low ranking of "poverty issues" suggests that they are concerned about economic conditions that may affect job opportunities but do not necessarily rank increased spending for poverty as the highest priority. Hispanics, although overwhelmingly Catholic, do not exhibit markedly different attitudes toward abortion than the general population. Nor do Hispanics differ greatly from the general populace in their attitudes about the U.S. role in Central America.

While the Hispanic vote has been marginal in national elections, it has been consistently high in some specific regions and cities, contributing to the elections of Hispanics for Congressional, state and local elective offices.

Several factors account for generally low levels of registration and voting among Hispanics, but the most important seem to be confusion about politics which are described as "too complicated" and the feeling that public officials "don't seem to care" about the minority. In addition, the concentration of Hispanics among those with lower levels of education, higher unemployment and lower paying occupations contributes to lower levels of participation.

45

CHAPTER IV

HISPANICS IN NATIONAL OFFICE

In the 1980's the Hispanic community of the United States has placed its confidence on conventional forms of electoral politics rather than on protest politics. Many will wonder whether the change in focus will manifest itself in greater political power and public policy beneficial to Hispanics. Attention will invariably focus on elected and appointed Hispanic officials at the national level and on organizations like the Congressional Hispanic Caucus to determine what kind of impact these office holders can have, individually and as a group. This will perhaps create expectations on those Hispanic leaders that cannot easily be realized and that could lead to disenchantment with them and with the American political system.

There has often been a tendency to equate political presence with political power; thus it is assumed that simply by electing Hispanics to office, benefits will begin to flow. Granted, election or appointment of Hispanics to national office is an important accomplishment, but it is also important to consider what these individual officials have accomplished or should accomplish. The reality of American political institutions such as Congress, with its norms such as seniority, is that it takes time to acquire political influence that will move the institution. It is important, therefore, that in evaluating the present and future status of Hispanics in national politics, the student consider the institutions in which they will have to operate.

Historical Sketch - Hispanics in Congress

It may come as some surprise that Hispanics have been represented in Congress since the middle of the 19th century. Jose Manuel Gallegos, a priest, was elected as New Mexico's first territorial delegate to Congress and began serving in 1853. Although he could not speak English, he was able to secure a $127,000 appropriation from Congress for territorial development.(1) In the next 60 years of territorial status, eight other Hispanics would represent New Mexico in Congress.(2) During their tenure these Hispanics made numerous and persistent efforts to secure statehood for New Mexico, that status finally achieved in 1912. Two years later New Mexico elected the first Hispanic, Benigno "B.C." Hernandez, to

47

its single seat in Congress. Congressman Hernandez thus became the first Hispanic to serve as a full-fledged member of Congress.(3) He served in the Sixty-fourth Congress (1915-16) and again in the Sixty-sixth Congress (1919-20). Nestor Montoya of Albuquerque was the second Hispanic to represent New Mexico, serving in the Sixty-seventh Congress (1921-22).(4)

In 1929, Octaviano A. Larrazolo became the first Hispanic to serve in the U.S. Senate when he was elected to fill the unexpired term of Senator A. A. Jones who had died in office. Larrazolo, who had previously served as Governor of New Mexico (1919-20), was the first to espouse Hispanic interests before a national forum. In his first session in the Senate, he introduced a bill calling for the creation of an industrial school for Spanish-American boys; his speech in support of the bill won praise from several Senators and from Vice-President Charles G. Dawes. Failing health forced Senator Larrazolo to return to New Mexico where he died in 1930.(5)

Dionisio "Dennis" Chavez, who represented New Mexico in the U.S. House from 1931 to 1934 and was appointed to the U.S. Senate in 1935, was the first Hispanic to serve in both houses of Congress. Chavez served in the U.S. Senate longer than any other person in New Mexico's history, from 1934 until 1962, when he died in office. At the time of his death, Chavez ranked fourth in seniority in the Senate, was Chairman of the Senate Public Works Committee, a member of the Senate Appropriations Committee, and was clearly one of the most powerful senators in Washington. During his tenure Chavez sponsored legislation and pursued programs that were quite important for the state of New Mexico and for the Hispanic people. As a member of one of America's beleaguered minorities, Chavez was an early advocate of civil rights legislation. In 1944 he sponsored a bill calling for the creation of a Federal Fair Employment Practices Commission. For four years he labored only to see the bill defeated by a staunchly conservative Senate. He was a strong supporter of the 1957 Civil Rights Act, the first civil rights legislation since Reconstruction, which created a bi-partisan Civil Rights Commission to investigate civil rights violations and recommend new legislation. He also supported the 1960 Civil Rights Act which authorized the federal courts to appoint referees to help Blacks register to vote. Chavez was no longer in the Senate when Congress enacted the milestone Civil Rights Act of 1964 and the Voting Rights Act of 1965, but his earlier participation surely helped lay the basis for them. Chavez was also a strong advocate of organized labor and social legislation on behalf of the indigent, elderly and less privileged throughout his Senate tenure.

Working with Senator Chavez in Congress was Antonio "Tony" M. Fernandez who was elected to the U.S. House of Representatives from New Mexico in 1942. Fernandez represented New Mexico from 1942 until 1956 when he died in office.

Senator Chavez' death in 1962 cleared the way for another New Mexico Hispanic, Joseph M. Montoya, who had been elected to fill the vacancy left by the death of Congressman Antonio Fernandez. Montoya, who had just been re-elected to his fourth term in Congress when Chavez died, immediately planned a challenge against former Governor Edwin Mechem who had been appointed to succeed Chavez. In 1964 Montoya defeated Mechem to become New Mexico's third Hispanic U.S. Senator. Because his tenure spanned the activist period of the 1960's and 1970's, he was subjected to greater pressure from Hispanics to pursue Hispanic concerns than were his predecessors. Montoya responded by sponsoring the Bilingual Education Act of 1968 and the amendments of 1974. He also sponsored the bill creating the Cabinet Committee on Opportunities for the Spanish Speaking, a bill for training of bilingual persons in the health professions, and a bill creating a commission on alien labor. Furthermore, Montoya was a strong supporter of the Voting Rights Act of 1965 and amendments of 1970 and 1975 and other civil rights legislation of the period. He was also a consistent supporter of social legislation benefitting minorities, the elderly, labor and consumers. Montoya was defeated in 1976 by political novice and former astronaut Harrison Schmitt.(6) Since Montoya's departure no Hispanic has served in the U.S. Senate.

Linda Chavez' Bid for the U.S. Senate in 1986

The prospects for Hispanics in the United States Senate received an unexpected and encouraging turn in February, 1986, when Linda Chavez, the highest ranking Hispanic in the Reagan White House, resigned her job as White House Director of Public Liaison in order to enter the race for U.S. Senator from Maryland, when the incumbent, Charles Mathias, announced his retirement. Chavez had begun her metoric rise in the Republican Party by serving as President Reagan's Staff Director

of the U.S. Civil Rights Commission. Linda Chavez, a
native of Albuquerque, New Mexico who later lived in
Colorado was a school teacher and later a staff member
for both the National Education Association (NEA) and
the American Federation of Teachers (AFT) in Washington, D.C. before joining the Department of Health,
Education and Welfare during the Carter Administration.
Despite her strong Democratic Party background, Chavez
joined the Reagan administration as Staff Director of
the Civil Rights Commission in 1983 under the sponsor-
ship of William Bennett.

Candidate Chavez launched a vigorous campaign for
the Republican nomination and at one time led her
closest competitor Richard Sullivan by a 3 to 1 margin
in a late summer newspaper poll. Sullivan later
withdrew from the race. On September 9 Chavez won the
Republican primary with a resounding 73 percent of the
vote and an eighty thousand vote margin over her
closest competitor Michael Shaefer who got 12 percent
of the vote. Chavez' victory set the stage for the
1986 General Election confrontation with Democratic
U.S. Representative Barbara Mikulski who won the
Democratic nomination in an eight-candidate field. The
Chavez-Mikulski pairing marked only the second time in
U.S. history when two women faced each other in a U.S.
Senate race.

Chavez lost to Mikulski in the November 4, general
election despite an aggressive campaign in which she
called Mikulski a "San Francisco-style Democrat," and
"anti-male." Chavez, however, was hampered by her
recent residence in Maryland which contrasted with
Mikulski who was a native of East Baltimore. Mikulski
received 59 percent of the vote to Chavez' 41 percent.

Chavez' primary victory marked a unique turning
point for Hispanics in a state that had not been
particularly favorable to Republicans or Hispanics.(8)

Progress for Hispanics in the 1960's

The decade of the 1960's was an important turning
point for Hispanics in national politics. Prior to
this time only one or two Hispanics from New Mexico had
been elected to Congress. This changed in the 1960's
as several Hispanic Congressmen from other states
appeared on the scene. As these individuals were the
ones who organized the Congressional Hispanic Caucus
and have remained as the most prominent Hispanic
leaders in their respective states, it is appropriate

to review their political backgrounds and present status.

Henry Gonzales

One of the most colorful Hispanic politicians in the nation is Henry B. Gonzales, U.S. Representative from the 20th District in Texas. Gonzales was born in San Antonio, Texas in 1916. His parents, Leonides and Genoveva Gonzales, were both descendants of early Hispanic settlers in northern Mexico. Leonides Gonzales immigrated to San Antonio, Texas during the Mexican Revolution of 1910 where he published the Spanish language newspaper La Prensa. Henry Gonzales attended public schools in San Antonio, then enrolled at San Antonio Junior College. After studying engineering at the University of Texas at Austin, he returned to San Antonio and enrolled at St. Mary's University Law School. Although he received his law degree, he took a job as a juvenile probation officer. After serving in the Army during World War II, he returned to his job, eventually becoming Chief Probation Officer.

Gonzales sought his first public office in 1950, but lost in a race for State Representative. In 1953 he was elected to the San Antonio City Council. As a City Councilor he sponsored the ordinance that ended segregation in San Antonio recreational facilities. In 1956 he was elected to the Texas State Senate, becoming the first Hispanic to serve in that body. Gonzales quickly established his reputation with filibusters against discriminatory legislation in that body. He was elected to Congress in a special election in 1961 to fill an unexpired term, and has since been re-elected by resounding majorities, often running unopposed. Gonzales' 20th Congressional District is comprised of the heavily Hispanic heart of the city of San Antonio. In Congress, Gonzales is one of the highest ranking members of the House Banking, Finance and Urban Affairs Committee and is Chairman of the Subcommittee on Housing and Community Development.

Gonzales' greatest influence has been in the area of housing where he has been involved with the model cities legislation and amendments and in most public housing programs. He has also been a member of the House Small Business Committee and a zone whip for the House Democratic Party organization.(8) Gonzales has been a moderate Democratic Congressman on most issues except civil rights where he has been liberal. He has been a friend of labor, the poor, women and the elderly and has been an advocate of social security and social legislation. He was one of the original members and organizers of the Hispanic Congressional Caucus.

Edward Roybal

Edward Roybal is the most successful Hispanic politician in California's history. Born in New Mexico, Roybal moved to California at an early age and was raised in East Los Angeles. Roybal served at various times as a social worker, public health educator and administrator with the California Tuberculosis Association in the 1940's. He was one of the leading organizers of the Community Service Organization (CSO) and later the Mexican American Political Association (MAPA) in California. In 1949 he was elected to the Los Angeles City Council and remained in that body until 1962, at which time he was serving as President Pro-tempore of the Council. In 1962 he was elected to the 88th Congress from a Los Angeles district and has been re-elected ever since. Roybal is one of the ranking members of the House Appropriations Committee, chairing the Treasury, Postal Service and General Government Committee. He has also been a member of the Labor, Health and Human Services Committee and the Select Committee on Aging.

Congressman Roybal has probably been the most active Congressman in pursuing Hispanic affairs. He authored the Bilingual Education Act and sponsored legislation to extend and expand the Voting Rights Act. He also sponsored the work study program for low income students and legislation to provide community health centers. Further, he sponsored legislation requiring the U.S. Census and other government agencies to improve social, economic and health data for Hispanics. Roybal, a Democrat, has been a liberal in ideology and consistent supporter of civil rights, social security, and education legislation and is an advocate for minority workers and the elderly.

E. "Kika" de la Garza

Probably the singular most powerful Hispanic Congressman is E. "Kika" de la Garza, who serves as Chairman of the House Agriculture Committee. De la Garca was born in Mercedes, Texas, but attended public schools in Mission, Texas. He also attended Edinburg Junior College and later St. Mary's University, receiving his law degree in 1952. He served as an artillery officer in the U.S. Army during the Korean War. War. Returning to Texas after the Korean War, he served six terms in the Texas House of Representatives. He was elected to the 89th Congress in 1964 and has served in the House since 1965. De la Garza's 15th Congressional District includes the south Texas point cities of Mission, McAllen and Edinburg. This rich winter garden agricultural region forms an appropriate constituency for the Agriculture Committee chairman. The district also encompasses a large Hispanic population. Appointed to the House Agriculture Committee in his first term, de la Garza systematically served the committee in various sub-committees and acquired the needed seniority to be named Chairman in December, 1980.

A Democrat, de la Garza has been a moderate ideologically and a supporter of civil rights and social legislation. He has promoted increased control against drug smuggling, having served as a member of the House Select Committee on Narcotics Abuse and Control. De la Garza's primary work as a Congressman has been accomplished in his role as Chairman of the Agriculture Committee, where he is instrumental in establishing national agricultural policy. Since 1981 he has been involved in the passage of all major agricultural legislation, including the 1981 Omnibus Farm Act, initiatives to continue and improve the Farmers Home Administration's credit program for farmers, programs for rural development, and the food stamp program.(9).

Manuel Lujan, Jr.

The most divergent member of the Congressional Hispanic Caucus is Manuel Lujan, Jr. of New Mexico. He is the only Republican in the caucus and is an ardent conservative who frequently finds himself on the opposite side of issues from his caucus colleagues. Manuel Lujan, Jr. was born on May 12, 1928 in San Ildefonso, New Mexico, but grew up in Santa Fe where his father served as Mayor. Lujan attended St. Michael's High School, and following graduation from the College of Santa Fe with a degree in Business Administration, entered the family real estate and insurance businesses in Santa Fe and Albuquerque.

Lujan's first attempt at public office was in 1968 when he ran for U. S. Representative and was elected over the incumbent Democratic Congressman. Appointed to the Interior and Insular Affairs Committee, Lujan has risen to his present status as the top ranking Republican on the committee. Although he frequently finds himself as "odd man out" in Hispanic Caucus supported issues, Lujan's prominence as the highest elected Hispanic public official in the Republican Party carries added weight during Republican Party administrations. Lujan represented New Mexico's First Congressional District, with its heavy Hispanic concentration from 1968 until 1982 when New Mexico qualified for a 3rd Congressional seat. Since then he has represented the 1st Congressional District whose main composition is the Albuquerque metropolitan area.

Lujan's main goals as Congressman have related to his Interior Committee role. He was, for example, a sponsor of the Clean Air and Clean Water Act of 1970.(10) Lujan has steered a consistent conservative course in his opposition to social assistance and public employment and housing programs. His civil rights record is also spotty, although he did support bilingual education.

Robert Garcia

Robert A. Garcia, Congressman from the 21st Congressional District, the South Bronx in New York, is the only Puerto Rican and the only non-Mexican-American Hispanic presently serving as a full fledged member of Congress. (He was preceded by Herman Badillo, another Puerto Rican who represented the South Bronx in Congress. Badillo, the first Puerto Rican to be elected to Congress, was born in Puerto Rico.)

The son of the late Rev. Rafael Garcia, Robert A. Garcia attended Haaren High School, Brooklyn Community College, the City College of New York and the R.C.A. Institute. A decorated Korean War veteran, Garcia worked as a computer engineer with IBM prior to entering politics. Garcia served one year in the New York State Assembly and twelve years in the New York State Senate until 1979. As a State Senator, Garcia worked for prison and correctional reform and was deputy minority leader from 1975 to 1979.

Garcia was elected to Congress in 1979 and has been re-elected three times. In Congress Garcia has been very active in pursuing Hispanic interests on the legislative agenda. He introduced an amendment to the Civil Service Reform Act which sought to rectify underrepresentation of minorities in the U. S. Civil Service. He also secured the creation of an Office of

Bilingual Education within the U.S. Department of Education. As Chairman of the Congressional Hispanic Caucus, he played an active role in trying to increase Hispanic participation in politics and in efforts to forge a national Hispanic coalition from the various Hispanic groups in the United States. Garcia serves on the House Banking, Finance and Urban Affairs Committee.(11) He is a liberal Democrat who has been a supporter of minorities, the poor, laborers and the elderly.

Other Hispanics in Congress

In addition to the five Congressmen mentioned, there are two Hispanics who serve in Congress as Resident Commissioners for the American territories of Puerto Rico and the Virgin Islands. The Resident Commissioner serves as a delegate to Congress elected by the people of the territory to represent their interests. He may speak in the House and serve on committees but does not vote.

Baltasar Corrada, elected in 1976 to the 95th Congress as Resident Commissioner from Puerto Rico, was also an original member of the Congressional Hispanic Caucus. Corrada holds a B.A. and law degree from the University of Puerto Rico. A practicing attorney before entering politics, Corrada is a Democrat and serves in the House Education and Labor Committee.

Ron de Lugo, the present Resident Commissioner and delegate to the United States Congress from the Virgin Islands, is also the first person elected to that office in 1972. De Lugo was born in 1930 and was educated at St. Peter and Paul School in the Virgin Islands. He later attended Colegio San Jose in Puerto Rico before joining the Armed Forces where he was an announcer for the Armed Services Radio. He worked as an announcer for radio stations in St. Thomas and St. Croix, Virgin Islands. His first public office was as an at-large Senator in the Virgin Islands Legislature from 1955 to 1966. A Democrat, de Lugo represented the Virgin Islands as delegate to successive Democratic national conventions since 1956 and has served as a national committeeman. He was first elected as delegate to Congress in 1968 and to the 93rd Congress in 1972 when the position was finally created. De Lugo has been re-elected as delegate in every election except 1978 when he ran for Governor of the Virgin Islands and was defeated. In Congress de Lugo has divided his time between service in the House Interior,

Public Works and Transportation Committee and the Post Office/Civil Service Committees.

Hispanic Gains After the 1980 Census

Following the 1980 census, population changes resulted in substantial re-apportionment of U.S. House seats that proved beneficial to Sun Belt states. Population growth and shifts resulted in House redistricting that doubled Hispanic representation in Congress. It is therefore appropriate to review the circumstances that contributed to these new Hispanic victories and the Congressional districts they represent.

California

In California, the 4,500,000 Hispanics who make up 19.2 percent of the population also comprise one-third of the total Hispanic population in the United States. Most of these, or 80 percent, are Mexican-Americans. Despite the high population numbers, Hispanics have traditionally been underrepresented in national elective office. This is manifested by the fact that only one Hispanic, Edward Roybal, served as Congressman from California before 1982.

California qualified for two more Congressional seats as a result of the 1980 census, and the resultant redistricting created two "open" districts with no incumbent congressman, and restructured several others which forced at least one incumbent congressman to relocate. A third vacancy was created when an incumbent congressman did not seek re-election. The redistricting process in California was specifically designed to increase Democratic Party representation in Congress, but also had the effect of helping Hispanics. Because Hispanics were heavily concentrated in two of the above districts, they gained two of the three seats.(12)

A. 30th Congressional District. California's 30th Congressional District, represented by Democrat George Danielson for most of the 1970's, was changed considerably by the 1981 redistricting. The new district encompasses such suburban Los Angeles cities as El Monte, Alhambra, Monterey Park, San Gabriel, Montebello, Maywood, and Cudahy. Although once a rich agricultural area of orange, lemon and walnut groves, the district is now heavily industrialized with major manufacturing in rocket motors, automobile parts, and electronic components.

On June 8, 1982, a special election to fill the old 30th District seat vacated by Representative Danielson was held coinciding with the primary election for the new 30th seat. Matthew "Marty" Martinez, 53, a state assemblyman from Monterey Park (who was just completing his first term), was supported by the Waxman-Berman political machine and benefited from the heavy concentration of Hispanics, who make up 54 percent of the district's population. Martinez won the primary in a close race over Dennis Kazarian, who had been an aide to Representative Danielson. Martinez also won the special election with 32.4 percent of the votes over Kazarian, who received 29.1 percent, and Ralph Ramirez (a Republican), who received 15.9 percent, and two other opponents. Martinez won a special election runoff on July 13, 1982, with 51 percent of the vote over Ramirez, who received 40 percent. Martinez immediately flew to Washington and was sworn in on July 15, to serve the remaining 5.5 months of Representative Danielson's term and become the sixth voting member of the Congressional Hispanic Caucus. The victory gave Martinez the important advantage of incumbency in the district when he faced Republic Congressman John Rousselot, who had moved from the 26th District when the redistricting had placed him against another Republican. Martinez won the November 2 General Election with 54 percent of the vote over Rousselot, who received 46 percent, a margin of 8,975 votes. Martinez was re-elected in 1984.

B. 34th Congressional District. Another of California's new districts, the 34th, is also made up of suburban Los Angeles communities. The two largest cities in the district are located at different ends and contain about 80,000 people each. In the south is Norwalk, an older community made up of working-class people, about 40 percent of whom are Hispanics. On the other end is West Covina, a newer, still growing, and more affluent community. Also located in the district, whose population is 47 percent Hispanic, are Pico Rivera, La Puente and South El Monte.

Although the district was structured to provide a congressional base for one of several local Hispanic Democratic politicians, none entered the race. Initially, the only candidate was former three-time Congressman Jim Lloyd from West Covina, who received endorsement from the U. S. Chamber of Commerce and several Hispanic political leaders, including the mayors of Pico Rivera and La Puente. Eventually, Esteban Torres, a former White House official under Jimmy Carter and U.S. representative to UNESCO, entered the race. Although Torres' ties to East Los Angeles politicians concerned some Hispanic leaders in the suburban districts who viewed his entry in the race as an attempt by the Los Angeles "Taco Mafia" to take over the 34th District, the issue soon died down when many prominent Hispanics endorsed his candidacy. Torres drew support from organized labor, national Hispanic leaders and organizations, and other national Democratic leaders. Helped by such support and a vigorous campaign, Torres defeated Lloyd and a third candidate, Fred Anderson, in the June primary. Torres won convincingly in the November 2 General Election, receiving 57 percent of the vote to 43 percent for Paul Jackson, his Republican opponent, a margin of 17,500 votes. Torres was re-elected in the 1984 Congressional election.

Texas

Texas, where Hispanics number 2,900,000, or 21 percent of the state population, was the only state in 1982 with more than one Hispanic Congressman. Texas received three new seats as a result of the 1980 census, and the Texas State Legislature adopted a new congressional district map incorporating the three new seats on August 10, 1981. In this case the plan, recommended by Republican Governor William Clements and conservative Democrat House Speaker Billy Clayton, was pushed through the legislature by a coalition of conservative Democrats and Republicans.

On August 14, a group of Blacks and Hispanics filed suit in U. S. District Court claiming that the reapportionment plan discriminated against the voting rights of the two groups. Specifically at issue was the shaping of districts in south Texas, Dallas-Fort Worth, and Houston areas. Texas is one state where election law changes must conform to guidelines established by the 1965 Voting Rights Act; consequently, the federal court deferred action on the suit, pending review by the U.S. Department of Justice.

On January 29, the Justice Department issued a ruling that the new reapportionment improperly divided the Hispanic population in two south Texas districts, the 15th and the 27th. The legislature-appproved plan made the 15th District 52 percent Hispanic. The Justice Department maintained that the plan packed the

15th with Hispanics, while diluting their strength in the 27th.

When Governor Clements refused to call the legislature into special session to remedy the problem, the three-judge federal panel rearranged the two south Texas districts in February, virtually assuring that Hispanics would win both seats. Since popular Hispanic Congressman E. "Kika" de la Garza was the incumbent in the 15th District, the court's redistricting plan only helped assure his re-election.

A. The 27th District. The 27th District, one of three new Texas districts, is comprised of a strip of five counties lined up in the southeastern tip of Texas, stretching north and south along the coast of the Gulf of Mexico. At the northern tip is Corpus Christi and at the southern tip is Brownsville, the two largest cities in the district. The people of Brownsville were not too satisfied with the composition of the district as established by the court. There, residents have regarded the larger Corpus Christi as a traditional competitor for tourists and trade and were worried that their interests would take second place to those of Corpus Christi. Corpus Christi is the second largest (next to Houston) Texas seaport and has large petrochemical and aluminum plants and seafood processing. Brownsville, on the other hand, is more a Mexican-style city with a larger proportion of Hispanics. Export-import trade with Mexico is basic to the economy and it is a major agricultural producer of fruits and vegetables. Nueces (Corpus Christi) and Cameron (Brownsville) Counties have traditionally been supporters of the Democratic Party and, since the new distict was two-thirds Hispanic, it was tailor-made for a Hispanic Congressman.

In this district, Solomon P. Ortiz, the Nueces County Sheriff, a veteran of 18 years of public office-holding in Nueces County, entered the race, and as in the past, the working-class Hispanics provided the support needed for his electoral victory. In the primary, Ortiz faced a crowded field of candidates which included four Hispanics. Ortiz, who got 25.6 percent of the vote, narrowly defeated former State Representative Joe Salem, a popular Lebanese jeweler who speaks Spanish and is quite popular with Hispanics, by only 653 votes. Salem got 24.8 percent of the vote. Jorge Rangel, a young Harvard-educated attorney from Corpus Christi, ran an aggressive, well-financed media campaign, but ended up a distant third in the race with

18.5 percent. He was followed by State Representative Gerald Gonzales (17.3 percent) and Ruben Torres, a former state representative and chairman of the Texas Pardons and Parole Board, who got 13.8 percent. In the runoff election Ortiz received the endorsement of Torres, the only candidate from Cameron County, and by thus consolidating the Hispanic vote in the district, defeated Salem by almost 6,000 votes (Ortiz 56.2 percent to Salem 43.8). In the General Election Ortiz went on to defeat the Republican nominee Jason Luby, a former mayor of Corpus Christi, in a landslide. Ortiz received 65 percent to 35 percent for Luby, a margin of 31,350 votes. Ortiz won re-election in the 1984 Congressional elections.

B. The 23rd District. Another Texas district, the 23rd, also consisted of a Hispanic majority by 1982, but no Hispanic candidate emerged to challenge the incumbent veteran Democrat Representative Abraham Kazen, Jr. until 1984. In the spring Democratic primary, Bexar County Judge Albert Bustamante challenged Kazen in a campaign that stressed that the Hispanic majority needed a Hispanic representative. Bustamante defeated Kazen by 4,000 votes in Kazen's home county and by 15,000 votes district wide. Since Republicans had not contested the seat, Bustamante had no opposition in November. He thus represents the southern part of San Antonio and Bexar County in a district that is neighbored by that of his mentor Henry B. Gonzales. Bustamante, who grew up as a migrant worker, was a Junior High School teacher and football coach who entered politics in 1968 when he signed on as an assistant to Congressman Gonzales. In 1972 he was elected to the Bexar County Commission, but left in 1978 when he was elected as Bexar County Judge. Bustamante developed a reputation as a tough-minded judge with a penchant for publicity. Bustamante gained early distinction by winning selection as President of the 99th Congress Democratic freshman class, the first Hispanic so honored.(13) He also joined the Hispanic Caucus in 1985, becoming the 10th voting member of the caucus.

New Mexico

In New Mexico, Hispanics make up 36.6 percent of the state population, which is the largest percentage of any state. The New Mexico population increased by 28.1 percent between the 1970 and 1980 census. Thus, New Mexico also qualified for a new seat in the 98th Congress. As indicated earlier, Manuel Lujan had restored the Hispanic parity in Congress that had been the case throughout New Mexico history when he was elected in 1968.

Third Congressional District. Because the greatest population growth in New Mexico has been in the Albuquerque metropolitan area included in the old 1st Congressional District represented by Lujan, it was apparent to political demographers that one of the three new districts New Mexico was entitled to would be a metropolitan district which would serve the Albuquerque metropolitan area (Bernalillo County). Congressman Lujan, as a resident of Albuquerque, promptly announced that he would run from the metropolitan district. The only question that emerged during the reapportionment process regarding this district was which of the smaller counties near Bernalillo would be added to this central district to bring its population to approximately one-third of the state population. Torrance County was proposed in the original plan, but eventually De Baca and Guadalupe Counties were also included.

The boundary lines for the remaining two districts became a matter of controversy in the legislature. Although the historical, political and economic patterns of the state seemed to suggest that a northern district and a southern district were the most logical alternative, some conservative leaders in the legislature saw otherwise.

New Mexico has not only been characterized by its large Hispanic and Indian populations (Indians make up 8.1 percent of the population), but also because both populations are concentrated in the northern half of the state. These groups have also been characterized by low per capita income, higher unemployment, and greater dependence on social programs such as welfare and food stamps than other groups in the state. The north has also had a large corps of skilled and unskilled labor and small farmers. The southern half of the state, especially "Little Texas" in southeastern New Mexico, has been characterized by a greater Anglo concentration, and a more conservative orientation representative of large and medium-scale farming-ranching interests.

These traditional socioeconomic differences between the northern and southern half of the state have been reflected in political voting patterns. The north has supported liberal and moderate Democrats in national and state elections, while the south has supported

61

conservatives and Republicans.

With such clearly identifiable regional differences along ethnic, economic, and political lines, the redistricting process seemed to point to a north-south-central congressional district configuration. Predictably, however, the redistricting process was influenced by special and ideological interests.

Although Governor Bruce King had indicated in 1980 that the issue of congressional and state legislative reapportionment would be undertaken by a special session of the legislature sometime in late 1981 or early 1982 and after the final census figures were available, two congressional redistricting bills were introduced in the 1981 session of the legislature. One bill called for the division of the state into north-south-central congressional districts. Another bill called for the division of the state into east-west-central congressional districts. This latter bill was introduced by Representative Dan Berry, a leading member of the coalition of conservative Democrats and Republicans, who controlled the House of Representatives. This Berry Bill, which would have had the effect of splitting in two the heavy concentration of Hispanics in northern New Mexico, was adopted by the House Voters and Elections Committee and was passed by the House of Representatives. The state Senate, recognizing the controversial nature of the bill and the probability that it would be challenged in court by minorities (both because of the dilution of Hispanic votes and because census results were not yet complete), refused to take any action on the House-passed measure. Thus, the bill died when the legislature adjourned.

In January 1982, Governor King called the legislature into special session 10 days prior to the regular session in order to consider congressional and state legislative reapportionment. Governor King was clearly concerned that he might get a congressional reapportionment bill similar to the Berry plan which had passed the House the year before. Signaling that he would probably veto such a proposal, and indicating his own preference for a plan which respected traditional regional, social and political patterns, King presented his own reapportionment plan to the legislature.

The King plan was essentially a variation of the north-south-central district form, except that it divided the state almost diagonally, with boundaries for the two districts beginning near the northeast corner and running diagonally (along county lines) to the southwest corner of the state. The Hispanic and Indian concentrations were in the proposed northwest district and the Anglo-farming-ranching conservative interests fell in the southeast district.

Although at least five different plans were given serious consideration by the legislature, the basic contention was between the north-south-central district structure and the east-west-central district structure. Four of the plans were variations of the north-south-central plan, while the fifth was the Berry plan, which was reintroduced.

The debate on the measures, especially in the House of Representatives, was quite heated and bitter, with liberal Democrats condemning the Berry plan as discriminatory and a deliberate attempt to dilute Hispanic votes. Representative Berry retorted, with candid irony, that Hispanics were one-third of the state population and that his proposal give them one-third of the population in every district.

The debate on the measures reached a climax in the closing days of the special session when the Senate adopted a last-minute compromise bill prepared by Senator John Pinto (the only Indian in the Senate). The Pinto Bill, essentially a variation of the north-south-central district plan, offered a new twist in that it consolidated all the most Indian and Hispanic counties in the northern district, and it also placed Lincoln County in the northern district. Lincoln County was the home county of U.S. Congressman Joe Skeen, a Republican who had announced intentions of seeking re-election and had actively lobbied Republican state legislators to reject the Berry plan in favor of a north-south-central alternative. Alarmed at this new development, Skeen undoubtedly made known his displeasure to Republican legislators.

The House of Representatives meanwhile had adopted a slightly modified version of the Berry plan, which still retained one Hispanic county (San Miguel) in the southern district. When it became clear that neither house would accede to the other's version, a Joint House-Senate Conference Committee was created to iron out the differences in the bills. The conference committee arrived at a predictable compromise in which a trade-off of San Miguel and Lincoln Counties occurred. The Hispanic San Miguel County, along with

Harding County, went to the northern district, while Lincoln County and Grant County were restored to the southern district, thus satisfying the concerns of Congressman Skeen.

The compromise version of the bill was probably as satisfactory as could be expected for Hispanics, since only one county (Guadalupe, which had traditionally been part of the Hispanic coalition) was detached in the new districting map, which sacrificed it in the central metropolitan district.

The plan could not have been more ideally tailored for Bill Richardson, a political newcomer to New Mexico, who had established his credibility as a viable congressional candidate by running a very close race against Congressman Lujan in the 1980 election. Even before the new district boundaries were arrived at, Richardson had announced that he would be a candidate. Roberto Mondragon, the popular two-term lieutenant governor, also announced his candidacy along with District Judge George Perez and Santa Fe Attorney Tom Udall, a political novice in New Mexico who was trying to capitalize on his father Stuart and uncle Morris Udall's name recognition.

Although a newcomer to New Mexico, Bill Richardson assumed the lead in public opinion polls and built on it with an extensive media and personal campaign. Richardson, an Hispanic by virtue of his mother's Mexican background, made his ethnicity clearly known in Spanish-language television and radio announcements. An outgoing personality, Richardson devoted full-time to the campaign and for the first six months of 1982 was literally everywhere in the district. Richardson received over 60 percent of the delegate votes in the pre-primary convention and top position on the ballot. Lieutenant Governor Mondragon, although the better known candidate, was hampered by lack of finances for a strong media campaign, and his duties as lieutenant governor, which prevented him from devoting more time to the campaign. The result was that Richardson received the nomination over Mondragon by 3,488 votes. Richardson received 36.3 percent, Mondragon 30.1 percent, Perez 19.2 percent, and Udall 13.7 percent of the vote.

Having won the important Democratic primary, Richardson was able to run a more low-key campaign for the General Election against the little known Republican candidate, Marjorie Bell Chambers. He won the

November General Election overwhelmingly, receiving 64 percent of the vote to Chambers' 36 percent, a margin of almost 38,000 votes. Richardson was re-elected overwhelmingly in 1984 and in 1985 became the new chairman of the Congressional Hispanic Caucus.

As the 99th Congress convened in January 1985, the Congressional Hispanic Caucus (CHC), an organization of Hispanic Congressmen who speak for their Hispanic constituencies was comprised of twelve members including the ten full voting members and the two delegates from Puerto Rico and the Virgin Islands. Included in the caucus are the veteran Congressmen Roybal, Gonzales, de la Garza, Lujan and Garcia and the newcomers Richardson, Martinez, Torres, Ortiz and Bustamante.

The Congressional Hispanic Caucus

The Congressional Hispanic Caucus (CHC) was organized in 1977 even though some of its members had been in Congress since the 1960's. Even then, not all Hispanic Congressmen joined the caucus. Manuel Lujan for one was not an original member of the Caucus. The relatively recent formation of the CHC and its initial lack of full participation by all Hispanic Congressmen are symptomatic of the problems the caucus has continued to experience since its organization. The primary mover for the organization of the caucus was Herman Badillo, the Puerto Rican Congressman from New York, who saw it as a means to encourage greater unity among Hispanic groups in the U.S., as well as in Congress. The stated purpose of the caucus was "to monitor legislation and other government activity that affects Hispanics" and to "develop programs and other activities that would increase opportunities for Hispanics to participate in and contribute to the American political system."(14) It was founded in order to "reverse the national pattern of neglect, exclusion and indifference suffered for decades by Spanish-speaking citizens of the U.S." and to fulfill the need for the development of "a national policy on the Spanish-speaking."(15)

Despite such lofty statements, the CHC has had difficulty achieving the necessary agreement as to priorities, programs and policies that affect Hispanics. Consequently, the CHC has been unable to arrove arrive at a coherent national Hispanic policy, or to develop the necessary legislative agenda and unity to carry it out. Because of the different personalities, backgrounds and philosophies of the members, the caucus has had difficulty in presenting a united front. The caucus has been described by Washington correspondent Paul Wieck as "more of an informal arrangement than an organized group."(16) They were seen, according to Wieck, as a handful of independently minded members who had been in Congress a long time and who worked in tandem only when it was convenient. One manifestation of internal friction in the caucus occurred on May 5, 1983, as several Hispanic Congressmen were speaking in commemoration of "El Cinco de Mayo" a Mexican holiday commemorating the 1862 Mexican victory over the French in Puebla. Congressman Bill Richardson, wanting to make a special impression, spoke in Spanish, claiming it was a "first" in the history of the House. Congressman de la Garza disapproved of Richardson's action and criticized him for "pushing too hard."

Probably the most important victory of the caucus occurred in 1983 when several members actively lobbied against the Simpson-Mazzoli Immigration Bill. On October 5, 1983, House Speaker Thomas P. "Tip" O'Neill removed the bill from the House Calendar where it was scheduled for consideration. Two caucus members appeared in a press conference applauding the action and claiming it as "a major victory" and "the first cohesive win" for their diverse group. The caucus was subsequently criticized as an obstacle to immigration reform for vetoing the only solution being offered to address the national problem of illegal immigration. Even in this victory the caucus indicated differences of opinion among members. Congressman Manuel Lujan said, "everyone (in the caucus) is opposed to the Simpson-Mazzoli Bill, but each of us has different reasons."(17) Lujan, for example, will support only limited amnesty for aliens already in the U.S., while others regard amnesty as an essential aspect of reform. Moreover, Congressman Gonzales supports sanctions against employers who hire aliens while Lujan and Garcia are opposed. Even when the 99th Congress finally passed the Immigration Reform Bill of 1986 the caucus was unable to agree on a united position. Although the bill provided amnesty to illegal aliens in the country before 1982 as favored by some members, it also provided for penalties to employers who knowingly hire illegal aliens, a provision opposed by most members. Caucus members were able to push for some anti-discrimination safeguards, but overall the passage of the Reform Bill underscored the inability of the caucus to achieve consensus and a position of leadership in a policy matter of great concern to Hispanics.

Internally, some members have had difficulty

embracing caucus positions. Congressman Gonzales, for example, perceives that his role is to represent his district constituency, not serve as a regional or state spokesman for Hispanics. As the only Republican caucus member, Congressman Lujan has seen it as too oriented toward liberal programs and the Democratic Party, and has considered resigning for this reason. Garcia has favored the agenda of urban liberals (federal money for housing, education and jobs) as an appropriate caucus agenda which is probably acceptable to most members except Lujan and de la Garza. Because of these differences, the group has adopted a caucus rule that unless all members agree, no caucus position is adopted. Such a rule, of course, enables one congressmen to veto any proposal even if supported by all the remaining members.(18)

The intransigence of some of the veteran congressmen in advancing specific CHC objectives and goals may be altered by the five new members who have entered the caucus since 1982. These new Congressmen who have less individual power than the veteran members may want to use the caucus as a vehicle to greater serve the interests of their own districts as well as those of Hispanics nationwide.

The Congressional Hispanic Caucus as a Political Force (CHC)

As indicated before, the mere existence of Hispanic elected officials does not per se assure Hispanics of political power, though an organization such as the Congressional Hispanic Caucus (CHC) can certainly serve as a means to power. The history of the CHC would suggest that, measured by its own goals, it has not wielded much political influence. An analysis of the CHC, however, should consider the wider circumstances under which it wields political power, the limits of that power and the objectives it seeks. On this basis it is possible to evaluate the CHC on three levels, first as a unified political group operating within the Congress, second as a loose group of individual Congressmen who wield individual power which is beneficial to Hispanics, and third, as a collective group of Congressmen who wield collective influence as representatives of the Hispanic community in national politics.

On the first level, it is clear that aside from a fairly concerted effort in opposition to the Simpson-Mazzoli Bill, the CHC has not functioned as a unified group within the Congress. The inability of the caucus to present an alternative to Simpson-Mazzoli was an embarrassing admission by the members that they could not agree to an alternative proposal on immigration, even if they were united in their opposition to Simpson-Mazzoli.

A policy issue of concern to Hispanics and one that may test the influence of the CHC in national politics is the increasing number of states and communities adopting "English as official language" resolutions. Such resolutions which appeal to the nativistic preferences of WASP Americans are guised as supportive of core American values. Although the resolutions nominally call for recognizing English as the sole language to be used for public documents and conduct of official city business the implications for Hispanics are far greater. For example, it would preclude the printing of documents of any form in Spanish even if Hispanic population numbers would warrant it. It could also mean prohibitions against the use of Spanish by government officials in dialogue with Hispanic clients in need of social services, or the need to provide Spanish translation for Hispanic defendants in a court trial. By inference it could also threaten bilingual education programs throughout the country as a way of fostering an English only society.

By 1985 five states--Illinois, Indiana, Kentucky, Nebraska and Virginia--had passed such resolutions, and California overwhelmingly adopted a similar proposition in the November 4, 1986 election. On April 2, 1986 the city of Fillmore, California, half of whose population is Hispanic, became the first city to adopt such a resolution. There has even been talk of a possible Congressional resolution on the issue and if so the CHC will once again find itself tested as an effective bulwark on behalf of Hispanics.

The long-run effectiveness of the caucus will be determined by its ability not only to defeat proposals that are adverse to Hispanic interests, but also by its ability to present alternative proposals that have been developed by a cohesive caucus. It is apparent that the CHC presently lacks a decision-making mechanism to develop a coherent program of legislation for Hispanics for presentation to the Congress. In this respect, the unanimous consent rule which prevents the caucus from taking a position if one member objects could be counterproductive because one member can continually veto actions favored by the majority. In that situation the individual member is not obliged to seek compromise in return for his support because his single dissenting vote will prevent the caucus from acting. Development of a decision-making mechanism enforceable upon all the members is vital if the caucus is to operate as a viable group within the Congress.

Moreover, because of its small size and because of the importance of consensualism in the day-to-day operation of Congress, it is vital that the caucus present a united front on any issue it addresses. Even the slightest hint of internal dissent will greatly diminish its effectiveness in persuading other Congressmen that the caucus position truly represents the Hispanic position. The inability of the CHC to present a united front on a variety of issues deprives it of a very important strategic tool. The unity of the caucus in terms of actual members is insignificant, except in very close roll-call votes. Rather, the unity is important because of its potential influence on the other 425 Congressmen, some of whom may have sizable Hispanic constituencies or who may be sensitive to Hispanic concerns.

The caucus has already targeted many of these Congressmen by naming them honorary members of the caucus, but can probably improve the means used to communicate with them by a more formal process. Membership in the caucus has given members another informal group within the Congress where they can seek support for their individually sponsored bills; thus it is likely that a roll-call analysis would reveal a very high rate of congruence in the voting records of caucus members with the exception of Lujan. Thus we have the paradox of describing the CHC as a group which exhibits a high degree of congruence in voting and issue positions because of similar partisan, ideological and constituency interests, but not because of their membership in the caucus.

The CHC has probably functioned closer to the second level of analysis, that is, as a loose coalition of Congressmen who wield individual power. It is obvious that several of the veteran members, particularly Gonzales, Lujan and de la Garza never saw the caucus as more than a loose coalition and remained basically parochial in their loyalty to their home districts. Because they have achieved substantial seniority placing them in committee or subcommittee chairmanships or as ranking members, Congressmen de la Garza, Gonzales, Roybal and Lujan have been able to get things done for their constituents without tapping the resources or advantages offered by the caucus. It is difficult to quantify the exact number or quality of benefits received by Hispanics as a result of the efforts of these Congressmen because their work often benefits the public at large. It is axiomatic that their advocacy of programs or policies is based on a desire to help both their immediate district constituents (which include Hispanics) and the wider Hispanic community. Congressman de la Garza's role as Agriculture Committee chairman, for example, has produced farm policy and food stamp policy that has helped Hispanics as well as non-Hispanics. Congressman Gonzales' membership in the Banking, Finance and Urban Affairs and the Small Business Committees has produced benefits for Hispanic businessmen in San Antonio as well as those operating nationwide. Congressman Roybal's membership in the Appropriations Committee has contributed to government expenditures beneficial to Hispanics in Los Angeles and nationwide. Needless to say, the continuation of these Congressmen in office is important to the Hispanic community as their individual power will surely increase in proportion to their seniority.

On the third level of analysis, the CHC has not, as yet, achieved the desired visibility as a collective spokesman for Hispanic Americans. This is probably due to its lack of success in determining policy in a given area and to its inability to speak cohesively on any issue (except for Simpson-Mazzoli) due to its characteristic disunity.

Still, some progress has been made by the caucus in laying the basis for a collective national leadership of Hispanics. A permanent CHC staff is in place and has begun to perform a variety of services for member Congressmen and Hispanics. This staff will likely push for greater cooperation among Hispanic Congressmen and their staffs. A method of financing CHC activities has been established with the annual banquet held during Hispanic Heritage Week in September. A CHC Institute to coordinate the caucus' educational programs and other activities has been created. Finally, the CHC has gained visibility among Hispanic organizations and is recognized for its policy-making orientations in Washington. Moreover, the CHC Washington staff and the CHC Institute have begun to serve as a clearinghouse for collecting information on Hispanics. Its <u>National Directory of Hispanic Elected and Appointed Officials</u> and its <u>Guide to Hispanic</u>

70

Organizations are valuable resource materials.

In summary, the Congressional Hispanic Caucus has not achieved the level of influence hoped for by its organizers and desired by the Hispanic community. It is, however, still in its developmental stage and the entry of new Hispanic Congressmen may be the catalyst for change. One thing is certain; the potential for the development of the Hispanic community as a powerful political group hinges upon the successful transformation of the CHC into a leading Hispanic organization.

Hispanics In National Appointive Office

In 1980 the administration of President Jimmy Carter published A Directory of Hispanic Appointees in the Carter Administration.(19) The Directory was remarkable, not only because it was the first time there were sufficient Hispanics to warrant its publication, but also because it included what are comparatively high-level offices for Hispanics. Hispanics have for some time benefited from "Recognition Politics," a level of politics in which a particular group is recognized by the selection of one of its members to serve in an important government position. The key factor is that the group as a whole does not benefit; rather the individual singled out for a position stands for or symbolizes the whole group. Such appointments are of course accompanied by great fanfare and publicity. The extent of such recognition granted Hispanics has varied over time and among different Presidential administrations. Recognition politics has been a topic of much debate among minority political leaders. Critics contend that recognition is useless because only one minority person is selected to fill a position and because that single individual is incapable of making much of an impact in a vast bureaucracy. The persons selected, moreover, are not usually activists "in tune" with minority interests and problems, but are rather those considered "safe" by the appointing agency. Also, under the "revolving door" system, a single person who is regarded as safe is often appointed to sequential positions and thus is not in one position long enough to make an impact. A final criticism is that the single appointee may be part of a smokescreen to adversely affect a minority group. For example, appointing a conservative Hispanic as Director of the Civil Rights Commission may be seen as a way to undermine the commission's efforts for that group.

On the other hand, defenders of recognition

politics say it is important especially to a minority that has been largely ignored. Recognition is a manifestation that the granting authority acknowledges the importance of a target group. Although it is only one position, the feeling is that the presence of a minority member in a high-level position may alter his agency's perspective toward a specific minority and that better relations and services to the group may result. Recognition can serve as a source of esteem and pride for the minority group that comes from seeing one of their own in a high-level position. The appearance of Ramona Banuelos' name on American currency was seen as a source of distinction by Hispanics. Finally, there are instances in which the single minority appointee is able to make a significant contribution to the minority. Such has been the case with Thurgood Marshal, whose role as Solicitor General and later as Supreme Court Justice has resulted in his advocacy of policies favorable to the Black community.

Considered from the standpoint of the granting authority, the benefits of recognition politics (support from a large ethnic group) can be great, considering its small cost (one or a few positions in government). As for the minority, the importance of the recognition depends upon the level of the position granted and the degree or quality of contributions made by the appointee.

Richard Nixon was the first American president to use recognition politics as a way of attracting Hispanic voters support. Recognizing the importance of the Small Business Administration (SBA) to Hispanic enterprises, he appointed Hillary Sanchez as Director of the agency. Later, he selected Ramona Banuelos, an Hispanic businesswoman, to serve as U.S. Treasurer. Both appointments were advantageous to the Nixon administration; while acknowledging the Hispanic people as a group, it further advanced the Republican objective of helping Hispanics partake of the free enterprise system.

Both appointees were "safe" from the Nixon perspective in that they were conservative and in tune with Republican Party economic policy. Banuelos' selection suggested to Hispanics and women that the Nixon administration was responsive to both groups and, as suggested, seeing her name on American currency was a source of esteem. In his tenure as Director of the SBA, Sanchez stressed greater responsiveness to minorities, especially Hispanics, and successfully steered

SBA loans in that direction. Nixon's appointment of a third Hispanic, Philip Sanchez, as head of the Office of Economic Opportunity was probably intended to deflate opposition, since Sanchez was to preside over the dismantling of the agency. The fact that a Hispanic was directly involved in reducing a vast social program helped tone down the criticism that Nixon would have faced.

During the administration of Jimmy Carter, Hispanics were accorded greater recognition than ever before or since. They held more positions and more high-level positions than in any previous administration. President Carter created the position of Special Assistant to the President for Hispanic Affairs, a job held by Esteban Torres (later a Congressman). From that position close to the President, Torres effectively lobbied for Hispanic policy and for further Hispanic appointments. With three Deputy Assistants, Torres developed an Hispanic bureaucracy within the Executive Office of the President. Alex Mercure was appointed by Carter as Assistant Secretary of Agriculture for Rural Development and during his tenure was able to advance the interests of Hispanic farmers in the Southwest as well as the interests of Hispanic farm workers. Victor Marrero served as Under Secretary for the Department of Housing and Urban Development and was able to work for better housing policy for urban Hispanics. Edward Hidalgo became the first Hispanic to serve as Secretary of the Navy and through his efforts, the Navy and other military branches stepped up Hispanic recruitment efforts. Richard Rios and Graciela Olivares served as Directors of the Community Services Administration and thereby oversaw the various remaining social programs of the old Office of Economic Opportunity. Jose P. Lucero was Director of the Office of Revenue Sharing in the Treasury Department and Armando Rodriguez was a member of the Equal Employment Opportunity Commission. Hispanics were also appointed to many administrative positions in the various executive departments. President Carter also appointed more Hispanics to high-level diplomatic positions than any predecessor. Abelardo Valdez served as Chief of Protocol, Mary-Luci Jaramillo served as Ambassador to Honduras, Raymond Gonzales as Ambassador to Ecuador, Julian Nava as Ambassador to Mexico and Fernando Rondon as Ambassador to Madagascar. Carter also appointed many Hispanics to the federal judiciary, including one U.S. Court of appeals judge and fifteen U.S. District judges. Three Hispanics also were appointed as U.S. Attorneys and five as U.S. Marshalls.(20)

The visibility of Hispanics declined markedly in the administration of President Ronald Reagan. There is no Hispanic in a cabinet or sub-cabinet-level position and the overall number of Hispanic appointees has decreased. Dr. John Hernandez who served as Assistant Secretary for the Environmental Protection Agency suffered from the adverse publicity that affected that embattled agency during Reagan's first term and eventually resigned. Henry Rivera, a young New Mexico attorney, was appointed by Reagan to the Federal Communications Commission and the aggressive Chairman has succeeded in pushing for fairer treatment of Hispanics in the communications industry. Following President Nixon's example, Reagan also appointed an Hispanic woman, Katherine D. Ortega as U.S. Treasurer. Though not overly inclined to appoint Hispanics, Reagan is sensitive to the political leverage that can be derived from using Hispanics in the right circumstances. Thus, his selection of Katherine D. Ortega to keynote the 1984 Republican National Convention was aimed at appealing to Hispanic and women voters. Her appearance as the keynote speaker was itself a precedent for Hispanics.

The dubious value of a Hispanic appointment to a high-level position during the tenure of a President who is a known adversary of social programs and human rights is seen in Reagan's appointment of Linda Chavez as Staff Director of the U.S. Civil Rights Commission. In January, 1984, Chavez proposed a redirection of the Civil Rights Commission away from its traditional minority advocacy and toward the conservative Reagan administration guidelines. Chavez recommended, for example, "a study" on affirmative action in college hiring and admissions to determine if it had led to reduced academic standards. She recommended cancellation of a study on the effect of student aid cutbacks on Black and Hispanic enrollments. Chavez also suggested a study to determine if bilingual education furthered the "isolation" of Hispanic students. She asked the Commission to review its support of "busing as a way of ending segregation of schools" and urged it to study the adverse consequences of affirmative action programs.(21) Thus in one swoop one Hispanic appointee to one of the most important federal commissions urged a reversal of some of the most important programs and policies achieved by Hispanics in American politics.

For her efforts on the Civil Rights Commission, Chavez was later appointed as director of the White House Office of Public Liaison, thus becoming the

highest ranking Hispanic in the Reagan administration
and the highest ranking woman in the White House
political staff. Chavez later resigned to run for the
U.S. Senate as indicated earlier in this chapter.

The advantage gained by Hispanics as a result of
such high-level appointments is probably marginal, even
in a progressive administration, and can, as in the
case of the Reagan administration, be quite counter
productive. Although the appointments do reflect an
effort of the Presidents to recognize Hispanics, their
long-range impact in terms of public policy for
Hispanics is limited because of the short tenure of the
appointments and because the appointees operated in
isolated cases. The Carter appointments, especially to
the judgeships were more important, as was the precedent of appointing several Hispanics as Ambassadors to
Hispanic countries.

Summary

Marked progress has been made by Hispanics since
the days when one or two Hispanics represented New
Mexico in Congress. In the 1960's several new Congressmen, Roybal from California, Gonzales and de la
Garza from Texas, Badillo from New York and Lujan from
New Mexico along with Senator Joseph Montoya firmly
established Hispanic representation in Congress. The
Congressional Hispanic Caucus created in 1977 has been
slow to develop and implement its Hispanic agenda, but
the infusion of new blood with the election of five
additional Congressmen in the 1980's may be the catalyst needed. Although the presence of Hispanics in
national office does not assure Hispanics of benefits,
the increasing seniority and power of Hispanic Congressmen will assure that Hispanic interests are
protected. The number and status of Hispanic appointed
officials has not been equalled since the Carter
administration and presently only a handful of
Hispanics serve in high government positions. In
short, Hispanic influence has yet to be felt in national politics even though a few Hispanic Congressmen
possess important individual power. To achieve greater
influence on the national scene, Hispanics will have to
mobilize more effectively as a national voting bloc.
This will improve their chances of securing Hispanic
appointments in critical national administrative
positions. At the same time the Hispanic Caucus must
weld the growing influence of veteran members with the
numbers of new Congressmen in developing a policy
agenda for Hispanic Americans. With Hispanic appointed

and elected officials working closely together at the national level, greater linkages with state and local officials are possible.

CHAPTER V

HISPANICS IN PUBLIC OFFICE - STATE AND LOCAL LEVELS

Contrasted with the dramatic progress of Blacks in office holding since the passage of the 1965 Voting Rights Act, Hispanic progress has been more limited and more recent. Until the 1970's Hispanic office holding was restricted to some legislative, county, municipal and school board positions in New Mexico and rather limited and isolated cases in Texas, California, Colorado and Arizona. Since the 1970's an increasing level of population, greater numbers of registered voters, increased political awareness and the combined effects of the 1965 and 1970 Voting Rights Acts have been improving the fortunes of Hispanics. This section will review the nature and extent of elective office holding by Hispanics historically and in the 1970's and will highlight some important recent Hispanic victories in state and local politics and their implications for the future.

Historical Sketches of Hispanic Office Holding at State and Local Levels

New Mexico has always been the exception to the low levels of voter participation and office holding which has generally been the case among Hispanics. Not only was New Mexico the first state to elect an Hispanic U.S. Senator and Congressman but it is also the only state that has had sustained representation by Hispanics in Congress, in state office, in the state legislature and in county and local offices since it became a state.(1) In this, New Mexico can be viewed not merely as an anomaly, but can serve as a model for Hispanic populations in other states.

An Hispanic, Ezequiel C. de Baca, was New Mexico's first Lieutenant Governor (serving from 1912 through 1915) and its second Governor, elected in 1916. Octaviano A. Larrazolo, a Mexican-born immigrant, became New Mexico's fourth Governor in 1919 and was later elected to the United States Senate. In addition to the many aforementioned Hispanics who served in both houses of Congress throughout New Mexico's history (see Chapter 4), several other Hispanics served in various state offices. Since 1912, they have averaged about 30 percent of the membership of both houses of the Legislature. Hispanics, moreover, have been well represented in county and municipal governments and school boards in New Mexico. In all circumstances the success of Hispanics in New Mexico state and local politics was made possible by high levels of participation and support from Hispanic voters.(2) Yet, during the 1970's New Mexico also experienced a new surge of political participation even beyond already high levels. In 1974 Jerry Apodaca became the first Hispanic since Larrazolo to win the governorship. His administration not only thrust him into the national political spotlight, but further, helped to focus more attention on Hispanics.(3) What was equally impressive about the four years (1975-1978) that Apodaca served as New Mexico's Governor was the fact that Hispanics also held five additional elective positions in New Mexico state government (Attorney General, Secretary of State, Land Commissioner, Corporation Commissioner and State Auditor) and two positions in the State Supreme Court and State Court of Appeals, respectively.(4)

In 1982 Toney Anaya became the fourth Hispanic and the second in recent history to be elected Governor of New Mexico. In 1983, the new Governor stepped in and quickly resolved a legislative leadership stalemate in the New Mexico Legislature and personally stewarded a new budget through the legislature that avoided a financial shortfall and economic crisis in New Mexico. Like Apodaca before him, the new position thrust Anaya into the spotlight as the highest ranking Hispanic office holder in the country. Anaya relished this new role as chief spokesman for American Hispanics and became quite visible, appearing on the television program "Meet the Press" as well as in the national magazines Time and Newsweek. In February of 1983, Anaya experimented with a strategy for an Hispanic coalition. known as "Hispanic Force '84," an effort aimed at mobilizing the Hispanic vote in time for the 1984 Presidential election. Anaya hosted a Santa Fe meeting of "Hispanic leaders" including among others Miami Mayor Maurice Ferre, LULAC President Tony Bonilla, Polly Barragan (Colorado State Senator and National Democratic Party Vice-chair) and Richard Alatorre, a California Assemblyman. Together the group formed "Hispanic Force '84," with Anaya as Chairman and adopted the broad objective of enhancing Hispanic influence in the 1984 Democratic Presidential Convention and election. Planned activities included fund-raising, voter registration drives, drafting recommendations on delegate selection to enhance Hispanic representation at the Democratic National Convention and drafting of Hispanic resolutions for inclusion in the Democratic Party Platform. The meeting was historic not only because it brought together important Hispanic leaders from different states, but also because they concurred on the group's organization and objectives. Unfortunately, the enthusiasm that led to its formation was insufficient to carry forth the actual implementation of its strategies and objectives. Each of the Hispanic leaders returned home to his/her own political problems, and though some efforts were made individually to revive the "spirit of Santa Fe," nothing was done to translate the meeting into an organization which would implement the announced objectives. Anaya, buoyed by the Santa Fe meeting, stepped up his national media blitz and in April, 1983 even campaigned among Hispanic voters for Harold Washington in his bid for Mayor of Chicago. Anaya's meteoric rise in national attention reached such heights by late 1983 that he was seriously identified as a potential Democratic Vice-Presidential candidate.

Meanwhile, Anaya's frequent trips out of state, his national media attention and especially his role as spokesman for Hispanics proved extremely annoying to his New Mexico constituency, especially those Anglos who had supported him. Speculation that Anaya was trying to build a base for a Vice-Presidential run or perhaps a cabinet-level appointment in a new Democratic administration further exacerbated Anaya's poor image at home. Public opinion polls reported Anaya's declining popularity rating and bumper stickers urging, "Call home, Toney!" and, "Does Toney Annoya?" ridiculed the Governor.(5) During January and February of 1984, an Anaya sponsored educational reform program was destroyed by the New Mexico Legislature which drastically cut education spending and rejected most of Anaya's other proposals.

In 1984 Anaya belatedly endorsed Walter Mondale for the Democratic nomination and actively campaigned for him among Hispanic voters in various Presidential primaries. In New Mexico Anaya's support proved to be of little efficacy as Mondale lost the June primary to Gary Hart. By the time of the national convention Mondale had clearly won the Democratic nomination. Anaya's stature had declined so much that he was given only a token appearance before the Democratic National Convention in a seconding speech. Hispanic fortunes in the Democratic Convention were buoyed by the emergence of Henry Cisneros, the Mexican-American Mayor of San Antonio as one of the most serious contenders as Mondale's Vice-Presidential running mate. This, combined with his appearance before the convention, thrust Cisneros into the role of "shining star" among Hispanic politicians, eclipsing Anaya.

The glaring failure of "Hispanic Force '84" to accomplish its goal of increasing influence on the 1984 Democratic Convention and the drastic results for its leader Toney Anaya underscores the difficulties faced by an aspiring Hispanic leader on the national scene. Certainly such an Hispanic politician will have to build a political base at the state or local level, but when he emerges beyond that level he faces the prospect, as Anaya did, of antagonizing his fickle constituency at home with no assurance that he will be accepted by the larger national constituency to which he is appealing.

Outside of New Mexico, Hispanics historically made frequent but mostly unsuccessful bids for state level office, even as some Hispanic Congressmen in Texas and California were establishing a strong and enduring political base.(6) The following historical sketches of past Hispanic participation in politics in different states reflects their limited political involvement while highlighting those exceptional cases where they achieved success.

Arizona

Raul Castro was elected Governor of Arizona in 1974 in what proved to be a unique situation. Castro, who was born in Sonora, Mexico, came to the United States in 1916 and settled with his parents in Tucson, Arizona. After attending law school at the University of Arizona at Tucson, he embarked on a long and distinguished public career that saw him serve as District Attorney for Pima County (1954-1958), Judge of the Superior Court (1958-1964) and as U.S. Ambassador first to El Salvador and later to Bolivia. He returned to Arizona and private law practice in 1969 and in 1974 surprised everyone by being nominated and elected Governor in what has to be one of the most conservative states in the Southwest. Although Castro received strong support from Arizona's Hispanics, especially those concentrated in south Tucson and central and east Phoenix, his victory reflected his support from conservatives and moderates in the Democratic Party. Unlike New Mexico, this one-time victory of Castro has not been duplicated before or since in Arizona. The only other political success enjoyed by Hispanics in Arizona has been at the local level, such as that accomplished under the American Coordinating Council on Political Education (ACCPE) when they elected five city council-men in Miami, Arizona in 1962.(7)

California

In California, Hispanic political activity was spearheaded by the Mexican-American Political Associa-tion (MAPA). Organized in Fresno, California in 1960 by some former members of the Community Service Organ-ization(8) such as Edward Roybal, MAPA sought to reverse the trend of Hispanic exclusion from California politics by registering Hispanic voters and encouraging more Hispanics to run for office. MAPA's efforts were aimed at the Democratic Party which they claimed had frustrated Edward Roybal's 1954 bid for Lieutenant Governor and Henry Lopez's bid for Secretary of State. MAPA's activities in the 1960's did prove helpful in the election of two Hispanic state assemblymen, three Superior Court Judges and three Municipal Court Judg-es.(9) Its greatest victory was, of course, the election of Roybal to Congress.

Texas

In Texas the first notable Hispanic political success resulted from the efforts of an organization known as the Political Association of Spanish-speaking Organizations (PASO). A remnant of the "Viva Kennedy" clubs which had been spawned in 1960 to support the presidential candidacy of John Kennedy, PASO became active in Texas cities with sizable Hispanic popula-tions. One success occurred in Crystal City, Texas where PASO won control of the mayor's position as well as two city council seats.

The success of PASO was repeated later in 1970 when La Raza Unida Party led by Jose Angel Gutierrez emerged as a new force in Hispanic politics. La Raza Unida Party (LRUP) grew out of a mass Chicano student walkout which virtually closed the Crystal City schools in 1969. The walkout, led by a group known as the Mexican American Youth Organization (MAYO), began in protest against school board policies and ended when the board capitulated. The success achieved by MAYO prompted leaders to organize La Raza Unida Party. Their success in registering new voters in 1970 placed the party on the rolls of three Texas counties. In April, 1970 Gutierrez and two other LRUP candidates were elected to the Crystal City School Board. These three, along with the remaining Hispanic members (a remnant of the PASO days), reorganized the board with Gutierrez as Chair and proceeded to enact a wide range of policies to serve the primarily Hispanic constituency. Included were policies introducing bilingual education, a free lunch program, suspension of culturally biased testing, introduction of culturally relevant curriculum and texts and hiring of more Hispanics to teaching and administrative posts. In the same year the party also won two city council seats in Crystal City, a mayoral position in Cotulla and a council seat in Carrizo Springs, Texas.

By June of 1972 LRUP's organizing efforts had progressed sufficiently to call the first state convention in San Antonio, Texas. With Gutierrez as keynote speaker, the 500 delegates from 25 Texas counties proceeded to name party leaders. Mario Campeon, Gutierrez' close ally from MAYO, became the Party Chairman. The party also selected a slate of candidates for Texas state office headed by gubernatorial candidate Ramsay Muniz, a lawyer and former football player at Baylor University. Acquiring sufficient signatures to place the party on the state ticket and in some counties proved a formidable task but the party achieved its goal. Muniz received 214,118 votes or 6.3 percent of the total votes cast, which qualified the party for the 1974 election. At the local level LRUP secured the election of Zavala County (Crystal City) Sheriff, County Attorney and a County Commission post.

In 1974 the party again called on Muniz for the Governor's race and this time he polled 93,295 votes. The party completed its control of Zavala County by winning the offices of County Judge, District Clerk, County Clerk, County Treasurer, two County Commission seats and three Justice of the Peace positions. Gutierrez was elected County Judge and Muniz carried the county in the Governor's race.

The success of LRUP in Zavala County was as dramatic as was its failure in state level efforts in Texas and at the national level. A national convention of LRUP which met in El Paso, Texas in 1972 established a party organization and selected officers headed by Gutierrez as National Chairman. The apparent unity of the some 3,000 "delegates" from 17 states was short-lived, however, as dissension within the ranks of the fledgling party soon became apparent following the convention. Rodolfo "Corky" Gonzales, the Colorado leader of LRUP who had challenged Gutierrez for the

leadership, led his group out of the LRUP coalition.
Gutierrez, never able to match his national success to
that of Zavala County, eventually retired to the domain
of south Texas politics.(10)

The rise and fall of LRUP in Texas proved to be a
valuable experience for Mexican-Americans in Texas as
many Hispanics were able to savor for the first time
the triumph of political success. Meanwhile, the
example of Crystal City has inspired Hispanics in other
Texas communities to enter the political arena, this
time under the banner of the traditional parties.

New York

The political fortunes of Puerto Ricans in New
York have not been as great as those of the Mexican-
Americans described above. Although there are, as
indicated earlier, over a million Puerto Ricans in New
York (about 10 percent of the population) only about 30
percent are registered to vote. This has meant that
relatively few Puerto Ricans have been represented in
New York City government in a few city council positions. Instead, the political success of Puerto Ricans
has been more closely entwined with single individuals.
The latest of these is Robert Garcia who represents the
21st District (the South Bronx) in Congress. Garcia is
the political heir of Herman Badillo, the first Puerto
Rican politician to achieve national stature. Badillo
was born in Caguas, Puerto Rico in 1929 and migrated to
New York as a youngster. Educated at City College of
New York and Brooklyn College where he received his law
degree in 1954, Badillo entered law practice in New
York in 1955. In 1962 he served in his first public
office as Deputy Commissioner of the New York City
Board of Real Estate. This was followed by service as
Commissioner of the New York City Department of Relocation (1962-1965). He then served as President of the
Borough of the Bronx from 1966 to 1969. Badillo was
elected to the 92nd Congress in 1970 from the 21st
District in the Bronx and served four terms through
1978. After Badillo's retirement from Congress, he
served as New York's Deputy Mayor for Management (1978)
and Deputy Mayor for Policy (1979). In 1983 he was
appointed as Chairman of the Governor's Commission on
Hispanic Affairs for the state of New York. He has
been in private law practice since 1981.(11)

Florida

Because of their relatively recent arrival in the

United States, Cuban-Americans have had less time to develop a long history of political participation. Already, however, because of their higher education and economic status, Cuban-Americans have begun to make their mark in Florida politics. They were a significant force in the elections of Maurice Ferre and Xavier Suarez in Miami, Robert Martinez in Tampa and Raul Martinez in Hialeah. That their influence will continue to be felt in state, county and municipal level offices in Florida is evident by Robert Martinez' victory in the Republican nomination for Governor.

Hispanic Elected Officials in the 1980's

As of 1985 there were 3,202 Hispanic elected officials (HEO) in the United States. This is an increase of 78 or 2.5 percent from the 1984 total of 3,128. In six of the states with the greatest number of Hispanic elected officials (Arizona, California, Florida, New Mexico, New York and Texas as shown in Table VI), the number of HEO's has increased by 1,579 or 123 percent in the twelve year period between 1973 and 1985.

The greatest increase in actual numbers of HEO's in the twelve year period was in Texas where 910 more Hispanics were in office in 1985 than in 1972. Part of the reason for the sharp increase in office holders in Texas is due to the fact that with 254 counties with 1,200 elected officials and over 12,000 municipal governments, Texas affords much more office holding than other states like California which has only 58 counties and 500 municipalities. Also, intensive voter registration drives following the elimination of many restrictive barriers in the last ten years have greatly increased the number of Hispanics seeking elective office. What is encouraging is that all states except New Mexico have seen increases of over 100 percent. New York increased its number of elected Hispanics by 550 percent even though the number of HEO's (55), is far below what it should be as a proportion of the population. Florida also increased by 238 percent even though its number of HEO's (31), is also far below what it should be. New Mexico only increased by 60 percent, but that is because of its already high number of elected officials. However, even there the 219 additional officials is a large increase. California has also made notable progress, increasing its number of HEO's by 235 or 102 percent.

TABLE VI

HISPANIC OFFICE HOLDERS BY SELECTED STATES

1973-1985

State	1973	1985	Number of Increase	% of Change
Arizona	95	231	136	+143%
California	231	460	235	+102%
Florida	13	44	31	+238%
New Mexico	366	584	219	+ 60%
New York	10	65	55	+550%
Texas	565	1,475	910	+161%
TOTAL	1,280	2,859	1,579	+123%

Source: NALEO Education Fund, The 1985 National Roster of Hispanic Elected Officials, xiii. and NALEO News Release, September 18, 1985.

Table VII shows that the number of HEO's is well distributed throughout the country, although many states have only one or a few Hispanic elected officials. The greatest concentration of HEO's is in the Southwestern states of Texas (1,425), New Mexico (584), California (460), Arizona (231) and Colorado (166). The three states of Texas, New Mexico and California, in fact, account for over 75 percent of the HEO's in the whole country. This is because Texas (20 percent) and California (30 percent) have the largest Hispanic populations and New Mexico has the highest proportion of Hispanics (37 percent) in its population. Midwestern states such as Illinois with 27 and Michigan with 17 are also beginning to see a rise in Hispanic elected officials.

The nature of elected offices currently held by Hispanics suggests a pattern that deserves analysis. Table VIII shows that the great majority (97 percent) of HEO's held office at the local level. This indicates that Hispanics have as yet been unable (outside of New Mexico) to make significant inroads in state and national office. On the other hand, it also indicates that there is a large pool of talented HEO's who are beginning to receive local-level training and experience in elective positions who may make further inroads into the national scene in the years to come. Table VIII also shows that by far the greatest number of HEO's are in school boards (37.9 percent), municipal government (32.6 percent), law enforcement/judicial positions (16.5 percent) and county government (9.15 percent).

One interesting statistic not reflected in Table VIII relates to the gender of HEO's. Stereotypes about Hispanic culture would suggest that few women participate in political affairs. The truth is that statistics on Hispanic voting indicate that more Hispanic women vote than men, and while the number of Hispanic women in public office are underrepresented, the proportion of Hispanic women to Hispanic men is the same as for the American population as a whole. Also, Hispanic women hold a higher percentage (15 percent) of elective offices than women in the national population (10 percent).

New Mexico was the only state with an Hispanic Governor (Toney Anaya) and with other state Hispanic elective officials. These include Clara Padilla Jones, Secretary of State, Albert Romero, State Auditor, Jim Baca, State Land Commissioner and Eric Serna as Corp-

TABLE VII

HISPANIC ELECTED OFFICIALS BY STATE, 1985

State	Hispanic Elected Officials
Arizona	231
California	460
Colorado	166
Connecticut	12
Florida	44
Hawaii	1
Illinois	27
Indiana	5
Iowa	2
Kansas	7
Louisiana	5
Massachusetts	3
Michigan	17
Minnesota	3
Missouri	3
Montana	9
Nebraska	3
Nevada	8
New Jersey	26
New Mexico	584
New York	65
Ohio	8
Oklahoma	1
Oregon	3
Pennsylvania	6
Rhode Island	3
Texas	1,475
Utah	5
Washington	14
Wisconsin	1
Wyoming	5
TOTAL	3,202

Source: NALEO Education Fund, 1984 Roster of Hispanic Elected Officials and NALEO News Release, September 18, 1985.

TABLE VIII

HISPANIC ELECTED OFFICIALS BY LEVEL OF GOVERNMENT

AND OFFICE HELD, 1985

	NUMBER	PERCENTAGE
FEDERAL LEVEL		
U.S. Senators	0	0
U.S. Representatives	11	2.5%[1]
STATE LEVEL		
Governors	1	2.0%[1]
State Executives	4	-
State Legislators	115	-
LOCAL LEVEL		
County Officials	292	9.15%[2]
Municipal Officials	1,041	32.6%
Law Enforcement/Judicial	527	16.5%
School Boards	1,212	37.9%
TOTAL	3,202	

Source: NALEO News Release, September 18, 1985.

[1]Represents percentage of total number of U.S. Representatives or Governors.

[2]Represents percentage of total number of HEO's.

poration Commissioner.

Of the various elective positions, service in the state legislature is particularly important because of its direct role in policy-making and as an entree to state and national office. Thus a review of HEO's in state legislatures is most appropriate.

Hispanics held a total of 115 legislative positions in the Untied States, spread out over thirteen states. New Mexico had the greatest number of Hispanics in its legislature with 12 of 42 members in the State Senate (28 percent) and 22 of 70 members of the House of Representatives (31 percent). Furthermore, Hispanics controlled powerful legislative positions; Rep. Ray Sanchez was Speaker of the House and Sen. Michael Alarid was Majority Leader of the State Senate. Arizona had the second highest proportion of Hispanics in its legislature; 6 of 30 Senators (20 percent) and 6 of 60 State Representatives (10 percent). Texas had 4 Hispanics in the 31-member Senate and 20 Hispanics in the 150-member House. California had 3 Hispanics in the 40-member Senate and 4 in the 80-member State Assembly. Colorado had 2 Hispanics in the 30-member Senate and 5 in the 65-member House of Representatives.

In New York the predominantly Puerto Rican community had 2 members in the State Senate (both from New York City) and 5 members in the State House of Representatives (also from New York City). In Florida, Cubans had elected four State Representatives, two from Miami and one each from Tampa and Hialeah. Kansas had one Hispanic in the State Senate and one in the State House of Representatives. Finally, Minnesota had one Hispanic State Senator and Washington, New Jersey, Connecticut and Illinois each had one member in the House of Representatives.

Regionally, the greatest concentration of Hispanic state legislators is among Mexican-Americans in the Southwest. Although Hispanics are underrepresented in all states, these numbers reflect an awareness of the importance of state legislative office both for policy-making and as stepping stones to higher elective office.

In Puerto Rico virtually all of the elected officers from the Governor to the Senate and House of Representatives are Puerto Ricans, as expected.

Surely, the most publicized gains achieved by HEO's in American politics in the 1980's have been in the recent mayoral elections, particularly those of Henry Cisneros in San Antonio and Federico Pena in Denver. Even these victories were accompanied by lesser known successes in municipal government.

As of 1985 there were eight Hispanic mayors in cities with populations over 30,000 and three in major metropolitan centers. These included Cisneros of San Antonio, Texas, Pena of Denver, Colorado and Xavier Suarez of Miami, Florida. On November 5, 1985 Suarez defeated another Hispanic, Maurice Ferre, who had been Miami mayor since 1973. Other Hispanic mayors included Emilio Hernandez of Brownsville, Texas; Robert Martinez of Tampa, Florida; Raul Martinez of Hialeah, Florida; Luis Montano of Santa Fe, New Mexico; and Dee Martinez of Farmington, New Mexico. These numbers of course reflect only a sampling of cities with the larger populations. California alone has eight Hispanic mayors in cities over 25,000 population and New Mexico has even more though with smaller municipal populations. In 1985 Jim Baca was one of two candidates in a field of eight who made the runoff in the race for Mayor of Albuquerque, New Mexico. Baca, ironically, received the endorsement of the usually anti-Hispanic Albuquerque Journal and of the Albuquerque Chamber of Commerce but was rejected by the Albuquerque LULAC chapter and most of Albuquerque's Hispanic political leaders who endorsed his Anglo opponent. Baca lost the race by only 2,000 votes and a margin of 51 to 49 percent.

Case Studies of Hispanic Elected Officials

A review of the case histories of the top Hispanic elected officials in state and local government is revealing not only because it relates the path to political success followed by these Hispanic leaders and what impact their victories will have for Hispanics in American politics, but it also reveals the extent to which Hispanic voters contributed to that success.

The following sketches of the backgrounds and political careers of the top Hispanic elected officials in American state and local government will reveal not only the diversity of their backgrounds, but will also identify common factors, considering that the individuals come from different Hispanic subgroups and regions of the country.

Toney Anaya

Toney Anaya was born in the small community of Moriarty, New Mexico, on April 29, 1941. Perhaps it was the traffic speeding along Route 66 and Interstate 40 near Moriarty that inspired the drive that would characterize Anaya throughout his life. After attending Moriarty public schools Anaya enrolled at New Mexico Highlands University but transferred to Georgetown University in Washington, D.C. where he received a B.S. degree in 1963. His stay in Washington was made possible by patronage jobs provided by New Mexico Hispanics, Senators Dennis Chavez and Joseph Montoya. Anaya would be one of several dozen Hispanic New Mexicans who would follow the pipeline to Washington and return to excel in New Mexico politics.(12) Anaya enrolled at American University Law School in 1963 and completed his law degree in 1967. He remained in Washington for three years as Legislative Counsel to Senator Montoya, and returned to New Mexico in 1970 to participate in Montoya's re-election campaign. In 1971 Anaya took a job as administrative assistant to newly elected Governor Bruce King and received his first direct exposure to state government and politics.

In 1974 after serving short stints as Santa Fe County Attorney and Assistant District Attorney, Anaya entered the race for New Mexico Attorney General. Anaya won the primary by a relatively narrow margin which was made possible by strong support (67 percent) from New Mexico's Hispanic voters.(13) Anaya proceeded to win the general election in a narrow victory, receiving 51 percent of the vote. Again, Anaya's victory was made possible by the strong support received from Hispanic voters. During the next four years Anaya not only transformed the office of Attorney General into an activist law enforcement agency but also established for himself a reputation as a tough and aggressive law and order advocate bent on ferreting out corruption in government. Some of his most visible targets were old-line Hispanic party bosses who had dominated party politics in northern New Mexico for years. These prosecutions earned Anaya great admiration from the Anglo community and media but also created bitter enemies among the influential party bosses.

In 1978 Anaya challenged incumbent Republican U.S. Senator Pete Domenici, and although he lost, his showing was impressive enough to encourage his later political career. Some argue that Anaya began his bid for Governor in 1978 with his defeat by Domenici, and indeed his Santa Fe law practice between 1978 and 1982 seemed little more than a front for an intensive run for the Governorship. Anaya formally announced his candidacy for Governor in 1981, a full year before the election and long before any of his would-be opponents. His organization was established and visible by the March pre-primary convention where he received endorsement from 56 percent of the delegates. One other opponent, Senate Majority Leader Aubrey Dunn received the requisite 20 percent support of the convention necessary to qualify for the June primary. Another opponent, Fabian Chavez, unable to qualify at the convention took a back door approach to the primary by securing enough petition signatures to also appear on the primary ballot. Chavez' candidacy was supported primarily by Rio Arriba County Chairman Emilio Naranjo who had been alienated by Anaya as Attorney General. Chavez was regarded as a "stooge" candidate who was supposed to draw valuable Hispanic votes away from Anaya. Notwithstanding this opposition and the more formidable bid of the respected Senator Aubrey Dunn, Anaya won the primary handily, receiving 57 percent of the vote to Dunn's 34 percent. Chavez' candidacy failed to distract Hispanic voters who gave Anaya 70 percent of their vote.

In the General Election, Anaya faced another formidable opponent in John Irick, a conservative Republican State Senator from Bernalillo County. Attempts to draw Anaya into personal attacks failed as Anaya retained his approach as an aggressive leader who would fight corruption and restore integrity in government. Concentrating on substantive, rather than personal issues, Anaya presented innovative plans for economic development and education reform for New Mexico. Ultimately, it was the aggressive, lawyery, clean-cut urbane appearance and dynamic personality of Anaya which contrasted with the "good old boy" image of John Irick that was the key factor in the election. Many New Mexicans, especially in metropolitan Albuquerque, had tired of the "good old boy" image of Governor Bruce King and many saw both the Democrat Aubrey Dunn and the Republican John Irick as cut from the same mold. Moreover, Anaya's extensive record of public service impressed many voters who yearned for a change from the "old-style" politics of Santa Fe.

Anaya's victory was accordingly quite unusual for a Democrat and even more unusual for a Hispanic

Democrat. He carried Bernalillo County (the metropolitan Albuquerque area) with 53 percent of the vote, a comfortable margin of over 9,000 votes. Democrats rarely win in Bernalillo County and usually strive to keep the margin of defeat in the county to less than 10,000 votes in order to win statewide. Combined with his victory in Bernalillo County, Anaya amassed a resounding majority in the Hispanic counties, receiving 73 percent of the vote and a margin of over 27,000 votes which enabled him to win statewide with 54 percent of the vote to Irick's 46 percent.(14)

Anaya began his term as Governor impressively by leading the legislature through an economic crisis that averted a serious state revenue shortfall in 1983. Soon after, however, his frequent absences from the state and his activist posture as leader of "Hispanics" proved unpopular at home, as suggested earlier. In addition to finding his educational reform and economic development proposals rejected by the legislature, Anaya's administration was riddled with investigations of irregularities in campaign finance and handling of disaster relief funds that resulted in indictments and resignations of several top state officials. Anaya himself was the object of a probe by the U.S. Internal Revenue, a federal grand jury and the U.S. Attorney's office in the waning days of his administration.

These difficulties clearly clouded Anaya's accomplishments as Governor. Anaya, although one of the most activist governors in New Mexico history, had to endure throughout his term an unprecedented conservative coalition control in both houses of the legislature and declining state revenues caused by a sagging economy. Nevertheless Anaya pushed continuously for educational reform and increased spending in education. He pushed for funding which would expand university participation in high-tech development. He established programs to shift the emphasis in corrections from incarceration to treatment and rehabilitation. He also maintained a strong record of appointments of minorities--Hispanics, Blacks, Indians and women--to state government positions and he helped steward construction projects throughout the state including the first veteran's nursing home in New Mexico.(15)

Whether Anaya can rebound from the aforementioned setbacks and resume his stature as the dynamic and charismatic Hispanic leader of the future remains to be seen, but the prospects at present do not seem encouraging. New Mexico's single term limitation precluded him from seeking re-election in 1986 and the latest polls reflected a low approval rating for his administration. Thus his prospects for another run at the Governorship in 1990 seem unlikely. A run for the U.S. Senate also is unlikely since the only position open for election in 1988 is currently held by a Democrat. A cabinet post in a Democratic presidential administration is a possibility, provided Anaya can maintain a high profile as a viable Hispanic leader in the next few years, but even this has been clouded by the aforementioned investigations.

Henry Cisneros

Even as the political fortunes of Toney Anaya appear to be somewhat in decline, those of another young, charismatic Hispanic leader have begun to shine. Henry G. Cisneros' resounding victories as Mayor of San Antonio have thrust him into prominence as the rising star among Hispanic leaders. The extent of his emergence onto the national political scene can best be demonstrated by the inclusion of his name among finalists from whom Walter Mondale ultimately selected his Vice-Presidential running mate just before the 1984 Democratic National Convention. Cisneros was featured in a segment of "60 Minutes" and this further focused on his leadership ability and accomplishments in San Antonio. Cisneros' appearance before the Democratic convention revealed to a national audience the charisma and leadership qualities that have impressed his San Antonio constituency.

San Antonio, once known as the city of the Alamo, has been transformed since it sponsored Hemisfair into one of the nation's fastest growing metropolitan areas and is now the tenth largest city in the country. The changing urban complexion of San Antonio, however, has not changed the strong Hispanic orientation of the city, which has produced such Hispanic leaders as Congressman Henry Gonzales. Still, the election of Henry Cisneros as Mayor in 1981 broke the long tradition of Anglo dominance of City Hall that had prevailed throughout the city's history.

Henry G. Cisneros was born in San Antonio on June 11, 1947, the oldest of five children of George and Elvira Cisneros. George Cisneros, whose family had been in San Antonio for several decades, worked as an administrator at Fort Sam Houston and was also a Colonel in the Army Reserve. Elvira's family immigrated to Texas in 1924. Cisneros' parents followed a strict regimen for their five children, restricting television viewing to weekends and requiring the children to spend afternoon hours between 1 and 4 engaged in some activity aimed at self-improvement. Cisneros read many books, built dozens of model planes and learned to play the piano, along with other projects.(16)

Cisneros attended public schools in San Antonio, then enrolled at Texas A & M where the mandatory military cadet training further enhanced Cisneros' strong sense of discipline and order. In 1969 he married Mary Alice Perez whom he had known since grade school. The Cisneros' have two daughters. Cisneros received a Master of Arts in Urban Planning from A & M, then moved to Washington, D.C. where he took a job as Assistant to the Executive Vice President of the National League of Cities. He also enrolled in the doctoral program at George Washington University. In 1971 at age 24 Cisneros received a White House fellowship and worked for a year as an assistant to Health, Education and Welfare Secretary Elliot Richardson. Cisneros received a Ford Foundation grant and spent two years at Harvard where he received a Master's degree in Public Administration. He returned to San Antonio and took a position as Assistant Professor of Public Administration at the San Antonio campus of the University of Texas. In 1976 he completed his Ph.D. in Public Administration at George Washington University.(17)

In 1975, eight months after returning to San Antonio, Cisneros was elected to the San Antonio City Council. His political mentor was his uncle, Ruben Muguia, himself a civic leader and printer. Cisneros' entry into San Antonio politics occurred at a time of growing Hispanic activism and participation in city politics. Years of neglect by the dominant Anglo leadership had left the heavily Hispanic west and south side sections of the city in poverty and neglect. Unpaved streets and lack of drainage created a quagmire during rainstorms and the Hispanic barrios also exhibited the traditional problems of poor housing, high crime and high unemployment. Cisneros' principle approach to the problems was to push for economic development. He was re-elected in 1977 and 1979, thus serving six full years in the City Council.(18)

In 1981 at the age of 33 Cisneros was elected Mayor of San Antonio, the tenth largest city in the

United States and the largest with an Hispanic mayor. He received 63 percent of the vote, a substantial portion of which came from the 54 percent Hispanic population of San Antonio. Although very young, Cisneros brought to the office the most impressive educational credentials possessed by any large city mayor.

During his first term Cisneros devoted his energies to unifying the sharply divided city, which had historically been split between the whites who dominated, the Hispanic majority and the Black minority (7 percent). Cisneros enlisted the support of all groups in a dialogue calling for economic development and new industry which would bring new jobs to San Antonio. He thus eschewed the traditional Democratic Party welfare approach to social problems.

Among his early accomplishments were persuading the University of Texas to establish an engineering school at its San Antonio campus. Cisneros also conceived the idea for a "high tech" high school where students could take concentrated math and science courses. These efforts at expanding technical education were in line with his hopes of linking San Antonio to Austin in a high tech corridor. His efforts in pushing for economic development resulted in the location of such high tech firms as Advanced Micro Devices, Farinon Electric, Tandy and Control Data Corporation in San Antonio.(19)

Cisneros' success at unifying the community and in economic development were evident by 1983 when he ran for re-election, as he received an overwhelming 94.1 percent of the vote. This time all sectors of San Antonio were unified in their endorsement of his administration.

Although San Antonio is administered by a City Manager, Cisneros dominates city politics. In addition to performing the traditional ceremonial role in receiving citizen requests, petitions and delegations, he frequently travels to other states promoting San Antonio to prospective industries. Still a Professor at the University of Texas, Cisneros cannot even collect the official Mayoral salary of $4,040 per year. Nonetheless, Cisneros has been a full-time mayor. In addition to serving as a good mediator among conflicting groups, he has sharpened his political talents. He is a very charismatic individual, handsome, tall, lean and fit, the typical appearance of a military type, a throwback, perhaps to his days as a military cadet. Cisneros reflects the new mold of Hispanic politician, urbane and sophisticated with an Eastern education, who speaks better English than Spanish. Nevertheless, he maintains his roots among San Antonio's Hispanics. He and his wife and daughters (Teresa and Mercedes) live in the same house where his grandfather lived, and his daughters attend the same schools he attended as a boy. Among his priorities as Mayor have been massive drainage and street improvement projects for the formerly ignored Hispanic barrios in the west and south sides.(20) He is also proud of the fact that new factories have been built in the depressed westside by Levi Strauss, Sprague Electric and Control Data. He is a skilled speaker, capable of adapting his standard speeches to a particular audience after a few preliminary inquiries, and he is much in demand as a speaker. Cisneros' style is characterized by a bit of self-deprecating humor he uses in starting a speech to an out-of-town audience. He says, "My name is Cisneros," pointing out that he has been introduced alternately as "Cisneurosis," "Cisnernose," and even "Sclerosis."

Although Cisneros' rising prominence in the Democratic Party has caused speculation that he will someday run for national office or some Texas state level office, he insists that his only goal is to be the best Mayor he can possibly be. In April, 1985 Cisneros was again re-elected Mayor, but his percentage of the total vote dropped to 73 percent, because he linked his re-election campaign to a controversial bond issue that raised taxes but will provide funds for streets, drainage, libraries and new police and fire stations. His long-range development project for San Antonio called "Target '90-Goals for San Antonio" is patterned after the Dallas development plan and suggests that Cisneros plans to stay on as San Antonio Mayor for the immediate future.(21) Simultaneously, his stature is recognized by national leaders. Cisneros was selected by Ronald Reagan in 1983 to serve on the Bi-partisan Commission on Central America, and when the Commission issued its report in 1984 he wrote his own dissenting opinion.

Considering his education, ability, charisma and popularity, it is understandable that San Antonio citizens wonder how long Cisneros will remain as Mayor before he seeks higher office. Considering that Texas has not been known for its receptivity to Hispanics in state politics, Cisneros' immediate options may not be as open as they appear, especially since Henry Gonzales and Albert Bustamante seem to have a firm grip on San Antonio's two seats in Congress. On the other hand, in view of his background, Cisneros may well become the first Hispanic to break the traditional anti-Hispanic mold in Texas politics. Cisneros may regard himself as a viable candidate for a Vice-Presidential nomination especially in view of the serious consideration of him for the position by Democratic Presidential nominee Walter Mondale in 1984. Certainly Cisneros has been playing the role of a national candidate as manifested by a multi-state campaign tour that saw him campaign for various congressional and state candidates in September, 1986. In New Mexico, Cisneros campaigned for Hispanic Congressman Bill Richardson and other Democratic candidates for state office. Considering his young age, Cisneros certainly has much time to decide on his future political career. In the meantime he remains one of the most articulate, able and promising Hispanic political leaders in the United States.

Federico Pena

If Henry Cisneros' victories in San Antonio affirmed the new mobilization and voting power of Hispanics, the election of Federico Pena as Mayor of Denver, Colorado, "the Mile High City," proved that an Hispanic candidate can win a top mayoral position in a city with only a marginal Hispanic population. Indeed as Newsweek described it, Pena "won less by capitalizing on his [Hispanic] heritage than by transcending it."(22) In a city where Hispanics comprise only 19 percent of the population and which has been known for its conservative traditions, Pena made history in May, 1983 by leading the incumbent Mayor Bill McNichols and five other candidates with 38 percent of the vote in the primary election. In the run-off election on June 21, Pena defeated long-time Denver District Attorney Dale Tooley, receiving 79,200 votes (51 percent) to Tooley's 74,100 (49 percent). Pena's victory is even more remarkable when one considers that he first visited Denver in 1972 and that a poll conducted in early 1983, shortly after he entered the race, showed that only 3 percent of the population sample had heard of him.

Federico Pena was born in Laredo, Texas on March 15, 1947, the third son of Gustavo and Lucila Pena. Although Pena's forebears were among the founders of Laredo and one of its leading political families, he spent little time in the city of his birth. Most of his childhood was spent in Brownsville, Texas where Gustavo moved the family shortly after Federico's birth. A graduate of Texas A & M University, Gustavo was an international textile trader. All the Pena children attended St. Joseph's Academy, a private Catholic school. Federico also attended the University of Texas at Austin where he earned his law degree in 1971. He then took a job as a legal assistant in El Paso and in 1972 traveled to Denver to visit his brother, then a student at the University of Denver Law School. Although considering a job in California, he remained in Denver and instead took a job as a staff lawyer for the Mexican American Legal Defense and Education Fund (MALDEF). In 1974 he left MALDEF and took a position as legal advisor to the Chicano Education Project (CEP), a group lobbying for bilingual education programs and more equitable financing in public schools.(23)

In 1978 Ruben Valdez, the Colorado state representative from District 5, a predominantly Hispanic district in Denver's northwest side, vacated his seat to accept an appointive position. Pena, having established himself among the Hispanic community through his MALDEF and CEP jobs, entered the race for the legislative seat and was elected. As a first term legislator Pena was an advocate of bilingual/bicultural education, tenant rights, citizen rights relative to law enforcement and senior citizens issues. His influence was limited, however, because of his status as a freshman legislator and as a member of the Democratic Party which was the minority in the House of Representatives. He was re-elected in 1980 by a large margin. When the new legislature convened, the Republicans resumed their majority control. Pena and other Democrats were annoyed that their own minority leader Bob Kirsch was siding with the Republican majority. Pena thus engineered a move to remove Kirsch as Democratic leader and as a result was himself elected to the position of minority leader. In his new position of leadership Pena fought for the familiar issues, but now from a "state" perspective rather than that of his own district. By the end of 1981 the Denver Post ranked Pena as one of the top ten legislators in the state.

Recognizing the vulnerability of Denver Mayor Bill McNichols in the upcoming Denver Mayoral election, Pena decided to challenge for the job, and formally entered the race on December 3, 1982. The greatest immediate challenge was to make himself known, as a poll conducted in early 1983 reported that Pena had a very low 3 percent recognition rating among Denver voters. Notwithstanding the incredible odds, Pena plunged headlong into the race. He would eventually develop an outstanding organization which would consist of over 3,000 volunteers. Pena conveyed an image as a young, dynamic and energetic leader and appealed to Denver's middle age, middle class voters with his slogan "Imagine a Great city." Fundraising efforts spread out as far as Chicago, New York, Washington, D.C., Los Angeles, Phoenix, and throughout New Mexico and Texas. Governors Toney Anaya of New Mexico and Bruce Babbit of Arizona campaigned for him in Denver, and San Antonio Mayor Henry Cisneros spoke at a fundraising dinner in Colorado Springs. One of Pena's objectives of consolidating the Denver Hispanic vote was jeopardized when a prominent Hispanic who owned the only Spanish-language radio station endorsed his opponent, Dale Tooley, but eventually Pena got the bulk of the Hispanic vote. In a three-day period just before the runoff election, the Southwest Voter Registration and Education Project registered over 6,000 new voters. Forging a coalition consisting of Hispanics, women, unions, environmentalists, businessmen and other minorities, Pena won both the initial race and the subsequent runoff election.(24)

Considering the liberal coalition that enabled Pena to win, it is surprising that his ethnic background did not emerge as an issue in the campaign. This is a tribute to both Pena's ability as well as to the people of Denver.

One hundred days after Pena took office, Denver's Rocky Mountain News proclaimed in a headline, "Pena style draws acclaim."(25) Its story went on to say that although his administration was proceeding slowly and cautiously, he won praise "from all quarters...for setting a new style and tone; for opening up a Mayor's office that had been shut tight for 20 years...Pena has reached out, and feeding off the energy of his march to power, brought together a fractionalized city..."(26)

A year after he took office, the Denver Post conducted a survey which showed that 61 percent of Denver's voters approved of his overall performance in office and that "the 37 year old Mayor appears more popular with voters today than when they elected him..."(27) In the poll Pena drew highest praise for making government more responsive to the needs of citizens, for reorganizing the police department, for promoting business growth and economic development, for his efforts in expanding Stapleton International Airport and for improving convention facilities and attracting conventions to Denver. He received less support for his efforts in reducing crime and air pollution in Denver. Although Pena had experienced some setbacks, including some initial conflict with the Denver city Council and complaints about delays in airport and convention center construction and the lack of progress in fighting pollution and crime, the general consensus was the Pena "was doing a good job" and that "people genuinely like him."(28)

Pena's personal perception of his administration remained positive in March, 1985 when he responded to a student's letter. He listed as continuing priorities: (1) making city government more responsive; (2) improving public safety; (3) enhancing the social and physical environment; (4) expanding planning capacity; and (5) strengthening Denver's economic base. He listed as accomplishments plans for a new convention center and airport, redevelopment of a part of Denver known as the Central Platte Valley, establishment of a Mental Health Commission and Women's Commission, improving policies for handling domestic violence, and the position of Denver as a potential site for a major league baseball team. He also retained his vision of Denver's future when he said, "We have worked hard to maintain that sense of personal empowerment on the part of the people of Denver...A prudent administration... can open itself up and assist the community in building a consensus about the direction of Denver's future."(29)

Invariably the "love affair" of Denver's citizens with their new Mayor will probably fade, and Pena will experience some of the troubles which beset all politicians. But for the present Pena has succeeded in giving the people of Denver a more positive and optimistic outlook about their city and their Mayor. Although Pena's precedent-setting election as Mayor cannot be attributed to Hispanic political power, it does reflect the greater level of political sophistication of the Hispanic politician in effectively appealing to a wide cross-section of voters.

Maurice Ferre

On first glance it is not surprising that Miami, Florida with its large Hispanic population (581,030) has had an Hispanic Mayor. What is surprising, however, is that Maurice Ferre, who was Miami Mayor from 1973 to 1985, is a Puerto Rican rather than Cuban, which has become the dominant ethnic group (70 percent) in Miami. Not until 1985 when Xavier Suarez was elected Mayor did Miami have its first Cuban mayor.

Like other cities, Miami is characterized by a diverse and unique political environment which has influenced its complex political life. Ferre's 1983 re-election to a sixth term as mayor of America's best known resort city was characterized by intense competition and rivalry between the sharply fractionalized groups in Miami--Whites, Blacks, Puerto Ricans and Cubans.

Maurice Antonio Ferre (whose last name is pronounced Fu-ray) was born in Ponce, Puerto Rico on June 23, 1935, the son of Jose A. and Florence (Salichs) Ferre. He and his wife Maria Mercedes have six children (four boys and two girls). Maurice Ferre, who migrated to the United States as a youngster, graduated from high school in Laurenceville, New Jersey in 1953, then studied architectural engineering at the University of Miami in Florida, receiving his degree in 1957. Ferre remained in Miami after graduation and was first elected to public office in 1966 when he was elected to the Florida House of Representatives. In 1968 he was elected to the Miami City Commission where he served until 1970. In 1973 he was elected Mayor and was re-elected six times.(30) Although Henry Cisneros has been credited as being the first Hispanic mayor of a major American city, that distinction goes to Ferre, who was elected eight years before Cisneros.

Although Miami has experienced growing political competition in the last two decades, the rivalry was brought into even sharper focus in the 1983 election as a large field of candidates representing many groups bid for the Mayor's position in the primary election. The principal candidates were the incumbent Ferre, Xavier Suarez who emerged as the leading Cuban candidate, and Les Brown, a Black activist leader. Ferre won the primary but failed to receive the required majority to be elected outright, which forced a runoff election a few days later. In the runoff election he was challenged by Suarez who had been the runner-up in the primary.

Les Brown, the defeated Black candidate, reflecting the paranoia which has engulfed Miamians since the great Cuban migration began, endorsed Ferre, commenting that, "a victory by Suarez would mean a Cuban takeover of City Hall."(31) Ferre thus built an electoral coalition involving Whites, Blacks and Puerto Ricans, or basically all non-Cuban groups, while Suarez' following was mainly Cuban. Ferre won the election, but by a lesser margin than before. Cubans, bitter over Brown's remarks and what apparently had been an Anti-Cuban election, vowed to challenge Ferre in 1985.

Meanwhile Ferre experienced continuing difficulties in his sixth term. In an effort to satisfy his broad coalition and to work with the Miami City Commission (which in Miami includes four other members besides the mayor) he was forced to play the role of referee, mediating between the competing factions represented by two Cubans on one side and the White and Black commissioners on the other. The result was a very "fluid and flexible" situation with the Mayor sometimes siding with the Cubans and at other times with the Black and White commissioners. As a result of the developments, Blacks felt they had been snubbed by Ferre after helping him win re-election. The Black community's disaffection with Ferre became even greater when he voted to fire City Manager Howard Gary, the highest ranking Black in Miami government. The decision to fire Gary itself reflected a new split in the Miami City Commission as the Hispanics voted to fire him while the Black and White commissioners voted to retain him. Ferre cast the tie breaking vote, siding in this instance with the two Cubans in firing Gary. In response, Blacks initiated a petition to recall Ferre and obtained 18,000 signatures. The petition, however, fell short of the 20,000 signatures needed to order a recall election.

Even as Ferre was able to forestall the recall action, it became clear that his 1985 re-election effort would be difficult, as Suarez continued in his efforts to develop the organization necessary to unseat the incumbent. The Gary incident greatly eroded Ferre's base of support among Blacks who had given him about 95 percent of their vote in the 1983 election. The extent of Ferre's loss of support became evident on November 5, 1985 when he was defeated in the primary election which saw two Cubans, Xavier Suarez (a lawyer) and Raul Masvidal (a banker) lead a field of eleven candidates. In the runoff election Suarez defeated Masvidal by almost 7,000 votes, a margin of 57 to 43 percent.(32)

Ferre's main accomplishments as Mayor of Miami in

his 12 year tenure were stimulating commercial development in downtown Miami with construction of several new hotels and expanding Miami's role as a center for international trade. Ferre improved conditions for minorities through alteration of minority procurement policies, civil service reforms and directives which increased minority representation in the Miami Police Department and in the city work force from 39 percent to 66 percent. He also pushed for revitalization of Miami's depressed areas, thus providing greater opportunity for minority business and creating improved living standards in Overton, Liberty City, Little Havana and Coconut Grove.

Miami's first Cuban Mayor Xavier Suarez was sworn into office on November 13, 1985. Suarez was a native of Las Villas, Cuba and a resident of Miami for ten years before his election. Suarez studied at Harvard where he received a Master's degree in Public Administration at the John F. Kennedy School of Government and a law degree at Harvard Law School. In 1984 he opened the Miami law office for the Louisville-based law firm of Barnett and Alagra and practiced law until his election. Suarez is a former member of the Dade County Criminal Justice Council and the Chairman of the Miami Affirmative Action Commission. He had been defeated by Mayor Ferre in 1983 in his first try for office.

Hispanic Mayors in Tampa and Hialeah, Florida

As indicated earlier, increasing migrations of Cubans into Florida has greatly altered the political complexion of the region. Although Cubans had not elected one of their own as Mayor of Miami where they are most heavily concentrated until 1985, their impact has been felt in at least two Florida cities, Hialeah and Tampa where they helped elect Hispanic mayors.

Raul C. Martinez is in many respects typical of the emerging Cuban politicians in Florida. He was born in Santiago, Cuba on March 6, 1949 and came to the United States in 1960 at the age of 11. He attended Dade County Public Schools, graduating from Miami Senior High School. He later attended Miami Dade Community College and Florida International University where he received his Bachelor of Arts Degree in Criminal Justice. Martinez, a naturalized citizen, founded a newspaper known as El Sol de Hialeah where he settled in 1969 and began public service as a member of the Minority Group Housing Committee and the Hialeah Personnel Board. In 1971 he was elected Councilman for the City of Hialeah where he served until 1981. Martinez was elected Mayor of Hialeah in November, 1981 and has been re-elected since. The position of Mayor in Hialeah calls for a strong mayor who is "administrative head" of city government, and has enabled Martinez to exert strong leadership in industrial development which has made Hialeah the fifth largest city in Florida.(33)

Bob Martinez' origins in Tampa, Florida precede the great Cuban migrations of the 1960's. Unlike his namesake Raul from Hialeah, Bob Martinez was born in Tampa, Florida on Christmas Day, 1934. He attended Hillsborough County public schools and graduated from Jefferson High School in Tampa. Later he attended the University of Tampa where he received a B.A. in Social Science in 1957. He later studied at the University of Illinois where he received a Master of Arts in Industrial Relations in 1964. Martinez returned to Tampa and became a successful restaurateur as President of Cafe Sevilla Spanish Restaurant. He subsequently became a member of the Board of Directors of Key Bank in Tampa. He has served in various local positions. He was elected as the Mayor of the City of Tampa in 1979 and was re-elected in 1983 to a four year term that was to expire in 1987.(34) In 1986, however, he entered the race for the Republican nomination for Governor of Florida. Martinez defeated former U.S. Representative Lou Frey in the September primary then upset the heavily favored Steve Pajcic in the general election becoming the first Hispanic Governor in the state's history and the first Republican since reconstruction. Martinez received 54 percent of the vote to Pajcic's 46 percent. Martinez is now the highest ranking Hispanic elected official in the United States.

Puerto Ricans in New York City Council

Although Puerto Ricans have been the least politicized of all Hispanic groups, they too have had their elected officials, as indicated before in the discussions of Herman Badillo and Robert Garcia. In 1985 three Puerto Ricans held positions in the New York City Council; they are Fernando Ferrer, Rafael Castaneira Colon and Victor L. Robles.

Fernando Ferrer was born on April 30, 1950 in the Bronx and attended Catholic schools, graduating from Cardinal Spellman High School in 1972. He graduated from New York University and worked as an urban planner. Ferrer served in various appointive positions in

New York City and specifically the Bronx. A liberal Democratic Party member, Ferrer was elected to the City Council in 1982 and represents the 13th District of the Bronx which includes West Farms, Twin Parks, Charlotte Street, Concourse, Fordham and part of Kingsbridge.(35)

Rafael Castaneira Colon was born in Venezuela, the son of Victor Castaneira and Carmen Colon, both missionaries from Puerto Rico. The family moved to the Bronx when Castaneira was six months old. After attending public schools in the Bronx, he served in the Navy during the Korean War. After the service he returned to the Bronx, working as a social worker. He was Deputy Director of the Puerto Rican Community Development Project from 1976 to 1978 and then was Director of the Mult-service Drug Abuse Program from 1978 through 1982. Castaneira Colon, a Democrat, was elected to the New York City Council in 1982 and represents the 11th District from the southeast Bronx.(36)

Victor Robles was born on July 15, 1945 in Fajardo, Puerto Rico. He is the son of the late Felix Robles, a municipal Assemblyman, and Aurea Montanez. He attended public schools in Brooklyn, graduating from Eli Whitney High in 1963. After spending some time in the U.S. Army (1966-1968) Robles served on the Congressional staff of U.S. Representative Shirley Chisholm. He served as a member of the New York State Assembly from 1979 through 1984. Robles, a Democrat, is the newest member of the New York City Council having entered in January, 1985. He represents the 27th District from Brooklyn which includes Bushwick, Williamsburg, East New York and Cypress HIlls.(37)

Hispanics and Urban Political Incorporation

In retrospect, the presence of Hispanic Mayors and Council members in municipal governments described in the preceding pages is impressive, especially when one considers that they were totally excluded from city governments only 25 years ago.

However, as indicated earlier, the mere presence of Hispanics in public office-holding does not in itself assure that meaningful changes in policies and programs favorable to Hispanics will result. Although comprehensive studies on the impact of Hispanic participation in city government are limited, some preliminary studies prvide some interesting findings.

One of the first studies on the subject was done

106

by Rufus Browning, Dale Marshall and David Tabb, entitled "Protest Is Not Enough: A Theory of Political Incorporation."(38) A study of political mobilization of Blacks and Hispanics in ten northern California cities, the effort was to develop a theory of political motivation and its significance for the minorities. The authors refer to "incorporation" as the key measure of minority involvement in the policy process. They found that the impact of minority presence in urban government did not in itself assure the two minorities of influence in the public policy making process. In some cities the minorities, although present in the council were excluded from the policy process. Rather, the minority's impact was greater in situations when they were part of a coalition that was able to dominate a city council. The authors found that Blacks achieved higher levels of incorporation than Hispanics in the cities studied, and that the usual coalition was between Blacks and a White-liberal group. Hispanics achieved influence in only one city, Sacramento, and then only as part of a multi-ethnic coalition of various minority groups. In places where the Black minority was incorporated, the authors found a high proportion of meaningful policy changes such as increased employment of minorities, creation of police review boards, greater minority representation in city boards and commissions, increases in minority business contracts with the city, increased minority oriented programs and greater responsiveness and sensitivity of municipal government in delivery of services to the minority community.(39) The importance of these findings, according to the authors, was that they demonstrate the possibilities for Blacks or Hispanics if they can become incorporated into the decision-making structure of a community.

In a related study "Biracial Coalition Politics in Los Angeles," (40) Raphe Sonnenshein found that although Hispanics constituted 27.5 percent of the population of Los Angeles--a seemingly ideal population to form a bi-racial coalition with Blacks who make up 16.7 percent--this has not occurred. Instead Blacks united in a bi-racial coalition with White liberals (principally Jews) to control Los Angeles politics. According to Sonnenshein, Hispanics have been much less successful than Blacks in winning political incorporation in Los Angeles. This is manifested by the fact that since 1972 when the liberal coalition took control, only in 1985 did the predominantely Hispanic 14th district elect an Hispanic, Richard Alatorre to the City Council. Before that the district had been represented by a White conservative. Thus, although Hispanics are a major minority group in Los Angeles, they have only recently become a minor force in the Black-liberal coalition that runs the city.(41) It is expected that the redistricting of the Council and the increasing political activity of Hispanics will increase their representation in the Council and that eventually they will become part of a multi-ethnic group running Los Angles.

In another related article, "Rainbow Coalitions in Four Big Cities: San Antonio, Denver, Chicago and Philadelphia,"(42) Carlos Munoz and Charles Henry found that a "Rainbow" coalition of Hispanics and Blacks is not necessarily indicated in cities with large Hispanic and Black populations. In San Antonio, the White business establishment has been the dominant force in Henry Cisneros' coalition even though there is a strong potential for a dominant coalition of Hispanics and Blacks. In Denver, Federico Pena's coalition has been dominated by White political and business elites; and although Hispanics and Blacks supported Pena, they have not been fully integrated into the dominant power structure. More progress has been made in Chicago where Mayor Harold Washington was elected under a "rainbow" coalition. His administration has done much to integrate Hispanics into various levels of the city power structure and organization.(43)

Finally, the city of Miami represents still another variation in urban political coalitions. There according to an article by Christopher Warren, John Stack and John Corbett, entitled "Minority Mobilization in An International City: Rivalry and Combat in Miami,"(44) polarization has developed between the two dominant ethnic minorities, Hispanics (mostly Cuban) and Blacks. In the Miami case the aggressive and enterprising Cubans have become rapidly incorporated into the local economy dominated by the White community. Thus the position of Blacks as the disadvantaged minority has precluded a possible coalition with Hispanics. Instead Blacks find themselves isolated in their struggle against a political structure dominated by White and Hispanic business elites.(45)

Most recent studies on Hispanic incorporation into the urban political power structure thus reflect an inconsistent pattern. On the other hand, Hispanics have begun to appear among the ranks of Mayors and City Councillors in American cities. However, there is little evidence that their presence has resulted in

meaningful political integration changes even in cities
cities with Hispanic Mayors where they constitute a
sizable minority group. Nevertheless it is evident
that Hispanics can become a greater force if they can
join bi-ethnic or multi-ethnic coalitions with either
Blacks or White liberal groups as dominant forces in
urban communities. The pattern established by Black
urban mobilization can certainly be followed by Hispanics who have just begun to climb the political ladder
in the urban environment.

Summary

This chapter has shown that the greatest political
success achieved by Hispanics has been at the state and
local levels of government. Historically, New Mexico
has always led other states with its high level of
Hispanic participation, and even in recent years has
produced the highest level Hispanic elected officials
in Governors Jerry Apodaca and Toney Anaya. Governor
Anaya, perhaps more than any other Hispanic politico,
tried to lay the basis for national Hispanic unity
through "Hispanic Force '84," but suffered politically
for his efforts. By and large Anaya's term of office
has been characterized by declining popularity, conflict with the New Mexico Legislature and unfavorable
media coverage.

In Arizona Raul Castro's tenure as governor was an
exception to the otherwise minimal participation of
Hispanics in that state's politics. In California and
Texas, MAPA and PASO were the earliest organizations
involved in Hispanic political mobilization. In Texas,
La Raza Unida Party yielded notable if temporary
success in Crystal City and Zavala County, Texas.
Among Puerto Ricans in New York, Herman Badillo was the
first successful politican, both as President of the
Bronx Borough and later as Congressman.

In the 1980's Hispanic legislative representation
has increased so that they are at least minimally
represented in thirteen states. The highest representation of Hispanics was in the southwestern states of
New Mexico, Arizona, Texas, California and Colorado,
but New York with seven and Florida with four also led
Hispanic representation in the state legislatures.

The respective case studies of New Mexico Governor
Toney Anaya and Mayors Henry Cisneros of San Antonio,
Federico Pena of Denver, Maurice Ferre of Miami, Raul
Martinez of Hialeah and Robert Martinez of Tampa, along

with the three New York City Councilmen, illustrated the diverse backgrounds, political careers, activities and records of some of the most prominent Hispanic elected officials in local government.

While Hispanic political influence at the national level of government may still be in question, the information presented in this chapter illustrates that their participation in state and local government is encouraging. Nevertheless, the mere presence of Hispanics in positions as Mayors and City Councils does not in itself guarantee favorable programs and policies for Hispanics. The need is for Hispanics to become participants in bi-ethnic or multi-ethnic coalitions that control urban government. Hispanics have reached the first rung on the ladder of political success and only increased mobilization and coalition building will assure greater success in the future.

CHAPTER VI

HISPANIC ORGANIZATIONS

Edgar Litt correctly identified the central importance of ethnic organizations when he said:

> The persistence of American ethnic politics
> can be traced, in part, to the activity of
> organizations capable of mobilizing ethnic
> sentiments for political objectives. In-
> deed without the existence of ethnic based
> organizations, it is doubtful that ethnic
> politics, as we know it, would have been
> with us for so many years.(1)

Hispanic organizations have been the vanguard of the Hispanic struggle for social, political and economic opportunity in the United States. They have been active in every environment--social, legal, political, religious, business and professional--and every level of government in addressing the problems and concerns of Hispanics.

Figure II illustrates the prominence of an ethnic organization in transforming what would be a relatively powerless "categoric"(2) group into a series of viable organizations involved in direct political action. The organizations are then capable of generating inputs (demands and expectations) into the political system, as demonstrated by the theoretical model in the Intro-duction.

There are two general functions performed by ethnic organizations. One is the advancement of group consciousness which leads to greater cohesion and political power; the other function is the provision of goods and services which address the needs and concerns of the minority. There are several ways in which the organization enhances group consciousness. The ethnic organization emphasizes core values such as history, culture and language. It employs symbols such as folk heroes, songs and emblems to encourage group identifi-cation. The organization also generates dialogue and provides other forums of communication enabling differ-ent segments of the group to identify with each other's problems. These forums also help groups find a common ground, generating resources and laying the ground rules for strategies of action. Ethnic organizations are frequently formed in specific business, occupation-al or legal environments. In these cases the organi-

FIGURE II

THE IMPORTANCE OF THE ETHNIC ORGANIZATION

THE ETHNIC ORGANIZATION

Takes ⟶

And Translates it Into

Which Make Specific Inputs
Into the Political System

Broad and Diverse
Categoric Groups
such as Hispanics

A Number of Pressure
Groups such as:

LULAC
American G.I. Forum
National Council of
   La Raza
National Association of
Latino Elected Officials
   (NALEO)
MALDEF
NEDA

```
I
N
P
U
T
S
```

```
The
Political
System
```

```
O
U
T
P
U
T
S
```

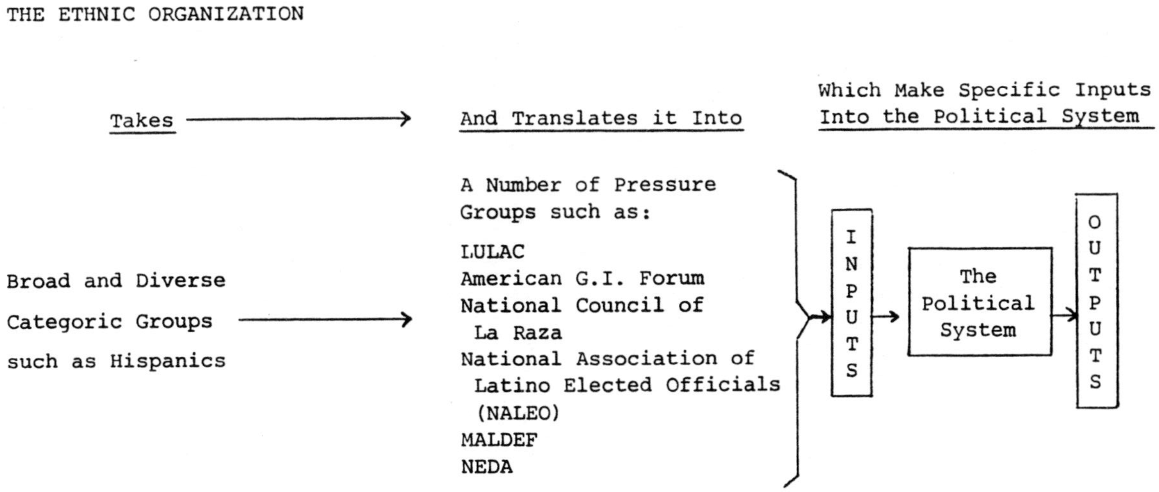

zation strives to improve the availability or delivery of specific types of services to the ethnic group. At the same time, these organizations strive to recruit minority members into that particular field so as to improve the services provided to the group.

Hispanic organizations, contrary to common assumptions, have been plentiful, but have faced inherent obstacles in advancing the interests of Hispanics. Among the difficulties have been the dearth of knowledgeable and skilled leadership, limited fiscal resources, and a constituency not always attuned to participatory democracy. In recent years all of these deficiencies have been somewhat ameliorated and some Hispanic organizations have begun to make significant progress. One continuing problem that follows when considering Hispanics as a collective entity is that up to now most Hispanic organizations have been formed around the particular Hispanic subgroup--Cubans, Mexican-Americans or Puerto Ricans. Fortunately, there is evidence that several Hispanic organizations have initiated efforts (as will be shown) to accomplish cross-group cohesion and consolidate their efforts in particular struggles.

Historical Development of Hispanic Organizations

The historical development of Hispanic organizations in some ways reflects the social and political experience of Hispanic groups in this country. That development can be divided into four main periods.(3)

The first period, beginning about 1846 with the American occupation of the Southwest and ending shortly after World War I, is broadly labeled the period of "Conflict and Apolitics." This period was characterized by bitter conflict over land and water and by hostile labor/management relations between Mexican-Americans and Anglo-American interlopers in the Southwest. Mexican landowners sought to protect their claims on the land secured through Spanish and Mexican land grants and recognized by the Treaty of Guadalupe Hidalgo. Arrayed against them were Anglo-American land speculators, large scale ranchers and farmers who visualized great fortunes because of unsettled and unclear land claims. The conflict often spilled over into violence as manifested by armed raids led by such Mexican chieftains as Juan Cortina and Juan Flores Salinas and the retaliatory campaigns of the Texas Rangers. Other examples of Mexican resistance were the exploits of Mexicans Tiburcio Vasquez and Joaquin

Murietta in California and Las Gorras Blancas in northern New Mexico. Later, as industrialization began to develop in the Southwest, Mexicans were perceived as a source of cheap labor. Conflicts between Anglo-American plant managers, mine owners, railroad managers and farm owners and their Mexican workers over wages, hours and working conditions also characterized the conflict of the first period. Hispanic labor unions such as <u>Confederacion</u> <u>de</u> <u>Uniones</u> <u>Obreros</u> <u>Mexicanos</u> (Confederation of Mexican Labor Unions) and <u>La</u> <u>Liga</u> <u>Obrera</u> <u>de</u> <u>Habla</u> <u>Espanol</u> (The Spanish Speaking Labor League) reflected the mutual aid and labor union character of those organizations. Along with their victimization in land claim adjudication and exploitation at work, during this period Hispanics began to be the focus of widespread discrimination and prejudice of Anglo-American society. Thus the group withdrew into itself, shunning any participation in political affairs and avoiding direct social contact with the external society.

Hispanic organizations of the period were essentially mutual aid societies which sought to protect and harbor the minority from the dominant society. An interesting fact of these organizations is the use of the term Hispano rather than the more specific group such as Mexican. Examples are the <u>Alianza</u> <u>Hispano-Americana</u>, <u>La</u> <u>Liga</u> <u>Protectera</u>, <u>La</u> <u>Sociedad</u> <u>Espanola</u> <u>de</u> <u>Beneficiencia</u> <u>Mutua</u> and even religious brotherhoods such as the <u>Sociedad</u> <u>de</u> <u>Nuestro</u> <u>Padre</u> <u>Jesus</u> <u>Nazareno</u> (the Penitentes) all of which provided mutual aid and benefit and also served as social outlets for their members. These organizations proved critical in preserving Hispanic culture, language and traditions during a very hostile period for Hispanic Americans.(4)

The second period, generally referred to as the period of "Accommodation," began in the 1920's and continued until the end of World War II. Like the preceding period, this period was one of great hostility toward Hispanics. The Spanish-American War contributed to American attitudes of suspicion toward Hispanics, whose loyalty was now questioned. Although Anglo hostility toward the Hispanic was confined to the predominant Mexican-American group in the first period, Puerto Ricans also began to suffer after 1900 as they appeared on the American scene.

During the second period, the Hispanic response to Anglo-American hostility was one of accommodation. The earliest organization to reflect the accommodationist temper was La Orden Hijos de America (The Order of Sons of the Americas) which was eventually succeeded by the League of United Latin American Citizens, or LULAC. These organizations asserted their loyalty to the United States, encouraged Hispanics to learn the English language, to prepare for American citizenship and to assimilate into Anglo-American culture. Like the accommodationist temper of Black leader Booker T. Washington, LULAC encouraged Hispanics to accept, at least temporarily, second-class status as a pre-condition to entering the mainstream of American life.(5)

The third, or "Politicization" period resulted from the combined changes wrought on the Hispanic community by the Second World War. As indicated before, World War II drastically altered the situation of Hispanics in the United States. Hispanic war veterans returning to the United States would no longer accept second- class citizenship status after receiving equal treatment in the military. Having proven their loyalty to the U.S. on the battlefield, they now demanded an end to the discrimination and prejudices they had faced before the war. Finally, the G.I. Bill provided heretofore unknown educational and employment opportunities. Hispanic organizations of this period thus reflected a more activist nature. In addition to encouraging Hispanics to register and vote, they were willing to use the courts to challenge discriminatory practices. LULAC abandoned its accommodationist policy and became a leader in litigation to remove discriminatory barriers in employment, education and public facilities against Hispanics. A new organization, the American G.I. Forum, modeled after the American Legion, also became active in civic action and reform for Hispanics. It was founded after a funeral home in Texas refused to handle the body of a Mexican-American, Felix Longoria, who had been killed in the Philippines. Incidents such as this, typical at the time, not only generated much publicity favorable to Hispanics but enabled LULAC and the G.I. Forum to expand rapidly in membership. Both organizations sought membership among all Hispanic groups and soon became national organizations with chapters in most states of the union. The National Puerto Rican Forum was organized in 1957 as the first Puerto Rican organization committed to improving job training and employment programs for Hispanics. In these postwar years a new group, the Community Service Organization (CSO) also emerged in California (1947). It emphasized community development in the style of Saul Alinsky and the Industrial Areas

Foundation. CSO sponsored voter registration drives and helped train such important Hispanic leaders as Edward Roybal, Cesar Chavez and Dolores Huerta. Political organizations such as the Mexican American Political Association (MAPA) in California, the Political Association of Spanish Speaking Organizations (PASO) in Texas and the American Coordinating Council on Political Education (ACCPE) in Arizona also emerged to further Hispanic political interests.

The more recent period in the political development of Hispanic organizations began in the mid-1960's as Hispanics sought to emulate the Black civil rights movement. Immediate attention focused on Blacks; the comparatively rapid response of government to the Black protest impressed Hispanic leaders who had been ignored for years. The result was an unprecedented activism among Hispanics manifested by groups such as Reies Lopez Tijerina's Alianza Federal de Mercedes (Federal Alliance of Land Grants) in New Mexico, Cesar Chavez' United Farm Workers Organizing Committee (UFWOC) in California and Rodolfo "Corky" Gonzales' Crusade for Justice in Denver. Tijerina engineered confrontations with the U.S. Forest Service by staging occupations in old "land grants." The Alianza's Tierra Amarilla courthouse raid received national attention. Chavez gained much national support for his boycotts against California growers and enjoyed the first successes in organizing farm workers. Gonzales protested police brutality and other forms of discrimination against Hispanics in the cities. These organizations and leaders spawned what became known as the "Chicano Movement." Hispanics picketed, boycotted, demonstrated and confronted authorities to challenge discrimination. Hispanic student organizations such as the Mexican American Youth Organization (MAYO) and Movimiento Estudantil Chicano de Aztlan (MECHA) continued the Hispanic struggle in communities and schools across the country.

In the early 1970's, La Raza Unida Party was organized in Crystal City, Texas, following a successful boycott of Crystal City schools launched by Jose Angel Gutierrez and MAYO. The group took control of the Crystal City School Board, municipal and county (Zavala) government and later competed in the Texas gubernatorial election. The party spread throughout the Southwest and held its first convention in El Paso, Texas, selecting Gutierrez as its first national chairman. In later years, the party declined due to internal differences and inability to expand its political base. Nevertheless, in its short life La Raza Unida was the most successful effort at organizing a separate Hispanic political party.

In the aftermath of the Chicano movement, Hispanic organizations proliferated during the 1970's and 1980's. The new organizations are not only more specialized in their orientation, but are more sophisticated in their organization and strategies.(6)

Classification and Examples of Contemporary Hispanic Organizations

In studying contemporary Hispanic organizations, the student is first impressed by their great number and diversity, contradicting the popularly held perception of Hispanics as a group which engages in limited organizational activity. For our purposes, an Hispanic organization is defined as a voluntary organization whose principal composition is drawn from people of Hispanic origins and which is engaged in activities that directly or indirectly advance the concerns and/or interests of Hispanics in American society. Thus, while most organizations described contain a specific focus, their effect is felt collectively by the larger Hispanic group or subgroup.

Funding sources, which often spell the difference between success or failure of an organization, are particularly important for an ethnic group such as Hispanics that has suffered from a shortage of capital to finance their diverse activities. There is nothing particularly remarkable about the funding sources for the many Hispanic organizations described in the following pages, except perhaps that many receive subsidies from federal government agencies such as the Minority Business Development Agency (MBDA) of the Department of Commerce, as well as the Departments of Health and Human Services (HHS), Housing and Urban Development (HUD) and Transportation. Private foundations such as the Ford Foundation, along with individual corporations such as General Motors, Ford, Xerox, Phillip Morris and others have also helped underwrite the Hispanic organizations' various activities.

Because of the many organizations involved, it is necessary to apply some arbitrary but useful classifications that will enhance comparisons and contrasts between organizations. First, it is important to note that some organizations mentioned are national in scope while others are more regional or local in orientation. Some represent Hispanics as a whole while others represent a more specific Hispanic subgroup.

National Civic Action Groups

It is appropriate to begin our discussion of Hispanic organizations with those that have made the largest impact on American society. The League of United Latin American Citizens (LULAC) is the oldest and largest Hispanic organization. Founded in 1927, LULAC is headquartered in Corpus Christi, Texas, and has chapters in 34 states. LULAC's broad goal is to unite efforts of civic action groups to assist Hispanic Americans. It has been involved in litigation on behalf of Hispanics to end discrimination in employment, education and public accommodations.

In recent years LULAC has been a frequent participant in boycotts involving varied Hispanic causes. In one recent example LULAC threatened a boycott against the H. E. Butt grocery chain in Texas alleging discriminatory employment practices. An agreement which prevented the boycott resulted in a five year affirmative action plan that will provide greater employment and training opportunities within the Butt Company and that established a $250,000 scholarship and training program for Hispanics.(7)

LULAC has also sponsored educational and employment programs for Hispanics. LULAC publishes the monthly LULAC News and holds an annual convention where national officers are elected.

The American G.I. Forum, founded in 1948, has served as a leading advocate for Hispanic issues, veteran's programs and civil rights. Among its programs for Hispanics are the veteran's outreach program, the education foundation, the National Economic Development program and Project SER-Jobs for Progress, co-sponsored with LULAC. At its peak the G.I. Forum had chapters in 23 states and over 20,000 members.

In recognition of the Forum's accomplishments as a civic action group, its founder, Dr. Hecter Garcia of Texas was awarded the American Medal of Freedom by President Ronald Reagan on March 26, 1984.

The Forum publishes a monthly newsletter, The Forumer and holds an annual convention where national officers are elected.(8)

The National Council of La Raza (NCLR) is a broad-based service organization comprised of 100 affiliated groups which have coalesced into NCLR to advance the social and economic well-being of Hispanics. It works for public policy, community assistance programs, special projects and media attention favorable to Hispanics. NCLR publishes a bi-monthly journal, Agenda, and holds an annual convention. NCLR's member organizations serve over 1 million people. It has a staff of 40 who work and operate out of three offices in Chicago, Phoenix and Albuquerque.(9)

Another effort to produce a coalition of Hispanic panic organizations is the National Forum of Hispanic Organizations formed in 1975. It is composed of 62 national Hispanic organizations whose representatives meet several times a year to develop and express a unified voice for Hispanics. The National Forum works to influence national policy for issues favorable to Hispanics, serves as a forum for discussing Hispanic issues and helps develop national strategies to advance Hispanic objectives.

The National Association of Latino Elected and Appointed Officials (NALEO) was established in 1975 to bring together Hispanic public officials in an effort to inform Hispanics of issues affecting them and to register Hispanic voters. NALEO has sought to utilize the strengths, resources and leadership of Hispanics in elected and appointive office to pursue public policies that are responsive to the Hispanic community. NALEO sponsors research, conferences, programs and information dissemination designed to increase awareness about Hispanics in American society and to increase civic and political participation within the group. Indeed one of the important contributions of NALEO is the publication of a National Roster of Hispanic Elected Officials which was a valuable resource used in Chapter 5 of this book. NALEO, headquartered in Washington, D.C., publishes a quarterly newsletter, "NALEO National Report" along with frequent news releases to keep its membership and the public informed about its ongoing activities and matters of concern to the Hispanic community.

In addition to the singular efforts of these specific organizations there are several cross-organizational coalitions that have been formed to combine the efforts of several organizations. Examples are the National Hispanic Higher Education Coalition, and the Hispanic American Coalition for Economic Revitalization (HACER).

Business Organizations

Recognizing that many of the socioeconomic problems of Hispanics stem from economic disadvantage attributable to insufficient capital resources, some Hispanic organizations have targeted economic development as a way to address the group's problems. Probably the largest Hispanic business organization is the U.S. Hispanic Chamber of Commerce, organized in 1979 to coordinate all state and local Hispanic chambers of commerce into a national organization. The Chamber, like its well known larger forerunner, serves to advocate the interests of business, except that its primary concern is directed toward Hispanic businesses. Examples of local chambers which may or may not be affiliated with the National Hispanic Chamber are the Arizona Mexican-American Chamber of Commerce, the Hispanic Chamber of Commerce of Mississippi, the Illinois Federation of Hispanic Chambers of Commerce, the Nevada Latin Chamber of Commerce, the Texas Association of Mexican-American Chambers of Commerce and the Greater Washington Ibero-American Chamber of Commerce.

Another business organization is the Hispanic American Coalition for Economic Revitalization (HACER), founded in 1978 with representatives from 12 states to promote economic development in American Hispanic communities. The Latin American Manufacturer's Association (LAMA) identifies Hispanic manufacturers and technical firms for participation in federal procurement programs and contracts.

Probably the most successful Hispanic business organization is the National Economic Development Association (NEDA). Formed in 1970, NEDA grew to a total of 25 offices in 14 states by 1981 with an annual budget of over $3 million. Funded by grants from the federal Minority Business Development Administration (MBDA) and the Small Business Administration, NEDA provides technical assistance to Hispanics developing new businesses as well as assisting the expansion of minority businesses.

Professional Associations

Another type of Hispanic organization are those that have developed in particular occupational fields. Again, their membership and leadership is primarily Hispanic and they endeavor to increase the representa-ation of Hispanics in that field and to improve the delivery of services provided by that group to Hispanics.

The Mexican-American Legal Defense and Education Fund (MALDEF) is probably the best known of the Hispanic professional organizations. Organized in 1968, MALDEF is the Hispanic counterpart of the NAACP, engaging in litigation on behalf of Hispanics. MALDEF, with its permanent corps of lawyers supplemented by a backup of volunteer attorneys, has engaged in many forms of lawsuits involving discrimination or segregation against Hispanics. The most common type of cases adjudicated by MALDEF involve discrimination in employment and education. Because of MALDEF's direct involvement in a wide variety of cases that have affected Hispanics and because of the limited space available in this chapter to explore in great detail the activities of all the organizations described here, a review of some of MALDEF's activities will illustrate the types of concerns that are or could be of interest to other Hispanic organizations.

Of the various educational issues MALDEF has been involved with and court cases which it has sponsored probably the most publicized and noteworthy was the case of <u>Tyler</u> v. <u>Doe</u>. In that issue the school board of Tyler, Texas tried to charge the children of illegal Mexican aliens for education received in Tyler public schools. The board was acting in conjunction with a 1975 Texas state law which stipulated that local school districts could not receive state funds to finance the education of children of illegal aliens. The law allowed school districts to bar attendance altogether or to charge the parents for the education.

Accordingly, the Tyler, Texas school board decided to charge the parents of some 40 Mexican children the sum of $1,000 per year per child. Poor and unable to pay the $1,000, all of the children dropped out of school. MALDEF filed suit on behalf of sixteen of those children claiming the law violated the equal protection clause of the 14th Amendment of the U.S. Constitution.

The state opposed the suit arguing that any person who is in the state illegally is technically not within the state's jurisdiction, thus the 14th Amendment did not apply.

The Supreme Court in 1982 ruled in favor of MALDEF

and the Mexican children, stating that the children of illegal aliens have an inherent right to free public education which is considered a fundamental national policy.(10)

In a more recent case MALDEF participated in a lawsuit against the San Jose, California United School District which charged that the school district discriminated against Hispanic students by means of segregation. Initially U.S. District Judge Robert Peckham ruled against the Hispanics, saying that while the district was ethnically imbalanced, the school board had acted "without segregative intent." An appeal to the U.S. 9th Circuit Court of appeals overturned Peckham's ruling saying that the school district "had intentionally kept Hispanic students segregated since 1962." The Court ordered the school to end segregation over a five-year period and cease school closures in Hispanic neighborhoods, and directed it to institute bilingual education and dropout prevention programs.(11)

MALDEF has also challenged unfair educational testing, and inequitable school finance formulas in various states.

MALDEF has moreover been an advocate of Hispanic employment rights. In one recent case MALDEF won a settlement on a discrimination suit filed against the western region of the National Park Service (NPS). The agreement called for the NPS to develop an affirmative action law aimed at hiring and promoting Hispanics at all levels of employment throughout the western region of the NPS. Hispanics who held 5.1 percent of the 2,500 jobs in the region were expected to improve to 28 percent of blue collar, 5.3 percent professional, 7.6 percent administrative and 11 percent of technical jobs. An added benefit was that the higher percentage of Hispanics in the NPS work force would enhance service to Hispanics using the national parks.

MALDEF has also been involved in cases involving voting rights, districting and gerrymandering. In 1985 MALDEF joined a law suit filed by the U.S. Department of Justice against the city of Los Angeles which charged that the 1982 Los Angeles City Council redistricting plan deliberately diluted the voting strength of the city's Hispanic voters. The suit noted that although 27 percent of Los Angeles' population was Hispanic, not one of its 15 council members was Hispanic. In an unrelated coincidental development,

Richard Alatorre, a California State Assemblyman, was elected to the Council in a special election, becoming the first Hispanic in the Los Angeles City Council in 23 years. On March 5, 1986 the Los Angeles City Council voted to re-apportion its voting districts in the wake of the federal lawsuit and in order to avoid further legal costs.(12)

MALDEF has also sponsored an extensive scholarship program to assist Hispanic law students attend school. The Puerto Rican counterpart of MALDEF is the Puerto Rican Defense and Education Fund. Formed in 1972, it has challenged discrimination against Hispanics in housing, education, employment, health care and voting. Closely related is the work of La Raza National Bar Association which encourages Hispanics to enter the law profession, works within the legislative process to promote Hispanic civil, rights and fights for cessation of police brutality. The Mexican American Law Students Association (MALSA) is composed of law students who help recruit Hispanics to law school, help them secure financial assistance and help them succeed in law study.

The engineering field is represented by such groups as the Association of Cuban Engineers, the Mexican-American Engineering Society (MAES), the Society of Spanish Engineers, Planners and Architects and the Society of Professional Hispanic Engineers. These organizations seek to advance the interests of Hispanic engineers in their profession and to encourage Hispanics striving for a career in the field.

Hispanic government employees are organized into such groups as the Association of Cuban Government Employees, the Chicano Correctional Workers Association and Incorporated Mexican-American Government Employees, Inc. (IMAGE). IMAGE seeks equal status and achievements for Hispanics in government work. Hispanics in media and broadcasting are represented by such groups as the <u>Club Hispano de Prensa</u> and the National Association of Spanish Broadcasters, which strive to advance Spanish media and the marketing profile of the Hispanic community. Hispanics in the health fields are represented by such groups as the National Association of Psychologists for La Raza which works to develop Hispanic psychology as a professional specialty within the American psychological community and to advocate psychological research, training and services for Hispanics. The National Association of Hispanic Nurses founded in 1974 has worked to improve health care in Hispanic communities and the National Coalition of Hispanic Mental Health and Human Services Organization has similarly worked to improve delivery of mental health and human services to Hispanics.

In the religious field the _Padres Asociados Para Derechos Religiosos, Educativos y Sociales_ (Associated Priests for Religiouis, Educational and Social Rights) or PADRES, the Spanish word for priests, is made up of Hispanics in the priesthood. This group has endeavored to alter Catholic Church policy to make it more responsive to its Hispanic clientele who comprise one-quarter of the 52 million Catholics in the United States. It has helped organize three national _encuentros_ (encounters) or conferences for Hispanic Catholic clergymen to discuss the status of the church relative to Hispanics and to urge new directions in church policy. It has also sought to increase the number of Hispanics in high echelon church positions such as Bishops. In 1970 there were no Hispanic bishops in the United States.(13) Since its formation, PADRES has effectively lobbied for the selection of seventeen new Hispanic bishops across the country.

The value of securing Hispanic appointments as Bishops is borne out by the tenure of the first such Hispanic appointed, Archbishop Robert F. Sanchez of New Mexico. In 1974 Sanchez became the youngest man appointed Bishop by Pope Paul VI who passed over several higher ranking priests. During his tenure the church in New Mexico has undergone changes which have reintroduced Hispanic cultural influences. Included are the use of the Spanish liturgy, revival of Hispanic religious celebrations or _funciones_, the use of Hispanic style vestments by priests and efforts to restore cooperation between Hispanic religious social organizations such as the Penitentes and the church. He has also encouraged greater lay ministerial involvement for young and old through retreats known as _encuentros_ or _cursillos_. Through these various endeavors the church has become an ally for Hispanics in retaining historical traditions and an advocate of cultural awareness.

Other efforts of PADRES have been the creation of national and regional Hispanic affairs offices within the Catholic Church, increased bilingual and bicultural instruction in seminaries and parochial schools, and increased efforts on human rights and justice for workers, farm workers and immigrants.(14)

Educational Organizations

A number of Hispanic educational groups have emerged, both to advance the interests of Hispanics in the education field and to promote better educational opportunity and special programs (e.g., bilingual education) for Hispanics. Aspira of America, a Puerto Rican organization primarily concentrated in the New York-New Jersey-Pennsylvania area seeks to improve educational opportunity for Hispanics. The Hispanic Higher Education Coalition represents 13 Hispanic organizations seeking improvement in post-secondary education for Hispanics. The group publishes position papers on Hispanic educational issues and provides testimony before Congress and educational commissions. The National Institute for Multicultural Education and the National Association for Bilingual Education (NABE) promote bilingual and multicultural education programs. They also strive for improvement of educational programs for Hispanics and recruitment of Hispanics into the teaching profession. The National Association for Chicano Studies (NACS) has, since 1972, sought to build Chicano political, cultural and educational awareness. Much of its effort is to improve and encourage research on Hispanics and to encouage dissemination of new findings in Hispanic history and culture. The Latin American Education Foundation has, since 1949, worked to provide better educational opportunities for Hispanic youth by providing scholarships and counseling programs.

Women's Groups

Hispanic women's groups have emerged to advance the particular interests of Hispanic women who suffer a dual minority status. Examples are Mexican American Women's National Association (MANA), organized in 1976 to advance the status of Mexican-American women and the Chicana Forum which is oriented toward advancing Chicanas in business and economic development. Another organization is the National Chicana Foundation whose main thrust is in education and career advancement of Hispanic women. The National Association of Cuban American Women (1972) and the National Conference of Puerto Rican Women (1972) have fought for equal rights for women of their specific groups and for Hispanic women in general. Both support the Equal Rights Amendment and seek to improve the status of Hispanic women in the nation's economic, social and political life.

Partisan Political Clubs

There are a number of Hispanic political organizations which have emerged to encourage Hispanic political participation. These groups have launched voter registration drives, have developed programs to advance Hispanic issues and have encouraged Hispanics to seek political office. Some of the groups have maintained independence from political parties while others have actively served the interests of and have been supported by one of the major parties.

The Mexican American Political Association (MAPA) is the oldest (1960) of the non-partisan Hispanic organizations. It has launched voter registration drives and supported Mexican-American candidates and issues. The Republican Party has made its appeals to Hispanics through groups like the Republican National Hispanic Assembly, the Mexican American Republicans of Texas and the Hispanic Republicans of Michigan, whose avowed aims are to recruit Hispanics to the Republican Party, to educate Hispanics about the American political process, to register Hispanic voters in the Republican Party and to support Republicans for office. Similarly, the Democratic Party has worked through such groups as the multi-state Hispanic American Democrats (HAD), Mexican-American Democrats of Texas (MAD) and the Michigan Spanish-Speaking Democrats, all of which have sought to increase Hispanic voter registration and support for the Democratic Party.

State Hispanic Councils

One development that is noteworthy, especially in Midwestern states, is the creation by state governments of special councils to advance the interests of Hispanics in state government. Since these advocacy groups take the form of lobbying organizations, they are worthy of mention. Examples are the Kansas Advisory Committee on Mexican American Affairs, the Maryland Governor's Commission on Hispanic Affairs, the Pennsylvania Governor's Council on the Hispanic Community, the Michigan Commission on Spanish-speaking Affairs, the Minnesota Spanish-speaking Council, the Nebraska Mexican-American Commission and the Illinois Spanish-speaking Peoples Study Commission. These commissions have made specific studies of Hispanic groups within their states and have made recommendations to state governments on public policies.

Local Civic Action Groups

Added to these special categories of Hispanic organizations are a plethora of local voluntary organizations which have advanced the interests of Hispanics in such diverse public policy areas as employment, education, law enforcement, health and housing. A few examples of such groups are the Latino Institute of Illinois, the Puerto Rican Congress of New Jersey, the Spanish-speaking Community of Maryland, the Tri-state Puerto Rican Congress, and the East Los Angeles Community Union.

Altogether the national, state and local organizations representing a variety of fields manifest not only the diversity of groups advocating Hispanic issues and concerns but also the maturation of the Hispanic community. Clearly, it would be to the advantage of the Hispanic community if some of these organizations would coalesce in their organizational efforts to avoid the obvious duplication of services and to better utilize the available resources. Nevertheless, there is little doubt that the Hispanic organizations described here are pivotal in the future political, economic and social development of Hispanics in American society.

Summary

This chapter described the importance of Hispanic organizations in mobilizing the Hispanic community and advancing its interests. It also described the types of organizations that represented Hispanics through the four periods of their political development. Finally, it provided a summary of the many types of organizations that have advanced Hispanic interests, with brief profiles given of the more important ones. Prominent among the groups are LULAC and G.I. Forum as general purpose civic action groups, MALDEF and the Puerto Rican Legal Defense Fund in the area of legal action, NEDA and local Hispanic Chambers of Commerce in the business fields, as well as various professional, educational, women's and partisan political organizations.

CHAPTER VII

PROSPECTS AND STRATEGIES:
NEW DIRECTIONS IN HISPANIC POLITICAL POWER

Hispanic politics, it should be clear by now, involves a struggle by Hispanics to participate in the formal and informal political institutions and processes that will avail to them a more equitable share of the economic and social resources of this country. Whether undertaken collectively or individually, all political activities engaged in by the Hispanics discussed in this book have been aimed at the above objectives. Until the 1970's the methods used in an attempt to achieve political influence involved protest, demonstration, boycott, picketing and litigation. Often the result was failure or defeat which occasionally vented itself in frustration and violence, but most often in isolation and despair. In the 1980's the methods have changed to more conventional accommodative styles of electoral politics. The main participants so far have been middle-class Hispanics who also have been the main beneficiaries; but their efforts at mobilization have compelled them to reach down to the masses of Hispanics for sustenance and support, thus introducing the broader Hispanic community to the political process.

The acquisition of political power for Hispanics has meant participating in the decision making process leading to desired programs and policies that would would otherwise not have been adopted. Have Hispanics achieved political influence in American politics? Considering an absolute definition of political influence, the answer would seem to be no. As a single group, Hispanics have not achieved national political power. Even in the fifty states, progress has been uneven. However, as noted in our earlier observations, Hispanics are not a monolithic group of people with a single leader or set of leaders embracing a single set of objectives. Instead they are an amorphous, diverse group with many leaders, many concerns and many program objectives. Political influence has been acquired individually and frequently vicariously by Hispanic leaders with varying levels of commitment to "Hispanic" problems and concerns. Some of these individuals such as the older members of the Congressional Hispanic Caucus, two recent New Mexico Governors and at least one Mayor have been able to attain some participation in the decision making process, but have been less successful in moving the governmental machinery to address specifically Hispanic problems. To an extent these Hispanic leaders have sponsored policies and programs that have been beneficial for Hispanics, but one of their glaring failures has been an inability to identify a set of issues, problems and concerns that would constitute an "Hispanic agenda" of policy and program priorities. Because of their diversity Hispanics have suffered from that lack of a single identifiable issue or a single national leader that would unite the group. Hispanic "national" leaders are essentially local leaders whose specific constituency has been limited to their specific group and region. The different subgroups in the Hispanic community have been very parochial both in their concerns and in their selection and support of leaders. These difficulties have obviously limited the potential importance that Hispanics could have in national politics because they have remained a politically fractionalized group. Indeed, the greatest success that has been enjoyed by Hispanics has been enjoyed by specific subgroups at the state and local levels. Accordingly, it appears that future Hispanic political influence will require political mobilization that begins at the grass roots among the different groups and evolves in the selection of regionally influential leaders who can establish the cross-group linkages that are necessary for a national Hispanic coalition. Some of the leaders and organizations discussed earlier have already initiated the process, even if their success has been limited.

Among the various topics and themes discussed in this book, several developments have become apparent and seem encouraging for the future of Hispanics and suggest possible strategies for future political change.

Probably the most encouraging development is that there is now an organized effort to register the millions of Hispanic voters who have remained outside of the American political process. A recent estimate placed the number of Hispanic registered voters at 3.4 million, less than 60 percent of eligible voters, as compared with 67 percent for the general population. An increase of at least one million would boost Hispanic registration above the national average. A National Hispanic Voter Registration Campaign was launched in San Antonio in 1983 with some 200 Hispanic leaders in attendance. The campaign sought to raise $2.4 million to support the drive which hoped to increase Hispanic registration by one million to 4.4 million voters.

Several factors suggest that the full impact of Hispanics as voters and as office holders in American politics has yet to be felt. First, the concentration of Hispanics in specific states and in specific regions of these states is significant. In California, for example, 50 percent of the Hispanic population is concentrated in 13 of the 45 congressional districts. In Florida, 50 percent of Hispanics are in 3 of the 19 congressional districts, and in Texas, 54 percent of Hispanics are in 5 of the 29 congressional districts.(1) If large Hispanic populations assure future increases in Hispanic elected officials, it is logical to assume that Hispanics will make congressional and local electoral gains in these districts. Second, data presented indicate that 40 percent of the Hispanic population was below the voting age during the 1980 census. Moreover, a substantial segment of Hispanics are in the 18 to 24 year old group which has been known to participate least in politics. As the Hispanic population ages the number of potential new voters will increase and participation in the process will also grow.

Finally, it has been shown that large numbers of legal resident aliens are Hispanics. Hispanic immigrants make up one-third of the Hispanic population in the United States, but the rate of naturalization is only 13 percent. Consequently, according to the 1980 census, 76 percent of Mexican immigrants, 55 percent of Cuban immigrants and almost 75 percent of immigrants from other Spanish-speaking countries had not become U.S. citizens. As these non-citizens complete the naturalization process, they will constitute still another untapped political resource for Hispanic voters and for future Hispanic elected officials.(2)

The success of the San Antonio-based Southwest Voter Registration Education Project and of the Midwest Voter Registration Project in registering new voters has already benefited candidates such as Democrat Governor Mark White in Texas and Mayor Harold Washington in Chicago, and has also contributed to the aforementioned Hispanic electoral victories. These two groups also combined with the voter registration drives of the National Puerto Rican Coalition and the Cuban National Planning Council to organize 300 voter registration drives in 28 states prior to the 1984 elections.

It has become clear that where voter registration drives have been conducted, Hispanic voters do see some relationship between their vote and the possibility that it can improve their life. Hispanic voters are more prone to register and vote if they perceive that economic and social benefits will result from their participation.

Financing, which had traditionally been a problem in Hispanic voter registration drives, has begun to appear from private foundations and some corporations such as Phillip Morris and Xerox.(3) In addition to new funding sources, recent electoral reforms such as the Voting Rights Act of 1970 and 1975, favorable court decisions, as well as state laws on such matters as gerrymandering, redistricting and registration procedures have helped reduce previous barriers to Hispanic voter registration.

It has also been demonstrated that advances made by Hispanics in voter registration and electoral reforms (such as reapportionment) translate into significant increases in the number of Hispanic elected officials. The increase in the number of Hispanic Congressmen after the 1980 census and reapportionment and the percentage overall increase in total Hispanic office holders in the United States verify this. It can be assumed that the presence of increasing numbers of Hispanic office holders in government will assure that their problems and issues of concern will receive greater attention.

Another encouraging trend has been the willingness of Hispanic leaders to campaign for each other and to make appearances in fund raising events. This has not only given Hispanic candidates at the local level new sources to tap for political support, but it enhances the visibility of an Hispanic from one locale in another part of the country. The appearance of Henry Cisneros in Colorado on behalf of mayoral candidate Federico Pena not only helped Pena, but it also exposed Coloradoans to Cisneros. A similar appearance by Cisneros in northern New Mexico on behalf of Congressman Bill Richardson in September, 1986 exposed Cisneros to New Mexicans and vice-versa. Surely the stature of a local leader such as Cisneros is greatly enhanced as a national spokesman for Hispanics when he has built alliances with Hispanic leaders in other states and can claim familiarity with the various segments of the Hispanic community. The appearances of Governor Anaya on behalf of Pena similarly served both purposes, while his support of Mayor Harold Washington of Chicago laid the basis for future coalitions between Blacks and

Hispanics. Increased contact between leaders of different Hispanic subgroups--Mexican-American, Puerto Ricans and Cuban-Americans--will also facilitate development of communication and dialogue which is necessary before biethnic coalitions are formed. Such coalitions are not only important in national campaigns, but also in the urban political environment.

The development of a new style Hispanic politician is another manifestation of the new Hispanic politics. Unlike the Hispanic politician of the past who depended solely upon Hispanics for his base of support, the new Hispanic politician is the young, urbane, middle class, college-educated professional, whether a lawyer like Anaya, Pena and Suarez, or an educator/urban planner such as Cisneros. This new aggressive, energetic, charismatic leader appeals to a broad cross-section of voters--whites, ethnics, women, businessmen and labor union representatives--for political support. Although his strongest support still comes from Hispanics, this new leader is also obligated to represent the other groups that make up his coalition of supporters.

The new Hispanic politicians have, however, frequently faced formidable obstacles and pitfalls uncommon to most politicians. Suspected and distrusted by an "Anglo" constituency that sometimes perceives them with some misgiving due to prevailing racial attitudes, Hispanic leaders have had to be overachievers in education, ability and professional experience to be legitimized by these Anglo voters. Even after the Anglo voter yields support to an Hispanic candidate, his tenure in office is subject to the greatest observation and scrutiny by the media lest there be any suspicion of wrongdoing or favoritism toward Hispanics. The Hispanic official's Anglo constituency is most fickle and unforgiving; its tenuous support, most difficult to acquire, may be easily and arbitrarily withdrawn. Hispanic elected officials find themselves constantly "on trial," their behavior judged according to certain prescribed standards. The difficulty is that an Hispanic candidate's support is frequently based on a precarious and diverse coalition that includes his own Hispanic people and many other groups. Much of the pressure comes from within his Hispanic constituency which sees his victory as an opportunity to right the centuries of wrong inflicted on Hispanics. Thus, no matter how many Hispanics he appoints to his administration or how many programs he institutes for the benefit of his people, he always faces the criticism of "not doing enough." The very nature of his diverse coalition makes it extremely difficult for him to satisfy all demands. If he appoints few Hispanics he is criticized for not doing enough, but if he appoints many then he is accused of favoritism toward Hispanics. The Hispanic politician thus needs to tread very lightly on matters pertaining to ethnicity. His very election to an important government position necessitates that he assume a position of leadership among Hispanics and that he express concern for Hispanic problems. Yet, if he becomes too active in this regard he risks alienation of his non-Hispanic constituency.

Also important in the new Hispanic politics are the new organizations which have emerged to advance the interests of Hispanics through traditional lobbying strategies or, as in the case of MALDEF, litigation in the courts. Such new organizations as the Congressional Hispanic Caucus, the National Hispanic Voter Registration Committee, The National Association of Latino Elected Officials (NALEO) and ASPIRA, along with traditional groups such as LULAC and the American G.I. Forum, have established a network of groups whose overriding concern for the economic, social and political interests of all Hispanics has not only enhanced the broader concept of Hispanics as a minority group in American politics, but has also laid the basis for greater cross-group cohesion among Hispanics. Considering the great emphasis placed on electoral politics in recent years, it is important to remember that there are other avenues to political change. As indicated before, Hispanic elected officials are limited in what they can accomplish. Much has been accomplished and will be accomplished by Hispanic organizations through direct pressure politics, protest politics and traditional lobbying methods. Indeed, many of the notable public policy advances which have resulted in direct economic, social and political benefits to Hispanics have been gained through non-electoral politics. Increased opportunity in education, removal of discriminatory barriers in employment, housing and social life, affirmative action programs and even political advances which have removed restrictions on registration and have reformed districting procedures are examples of policies that have resulted from pressure group activity in the courts, legislatures and the executive branches of government. A combined effort involving electoral and non-electoral strategies for political change is thus the most logical and pragmatic for Hispanics, given contemporary conditions and trends.

For Hispanics, the decade of the 1980's has signified not only a period of enormous political transition, but a greater source of optimism. There is, at long last, evidence of a surge in Hispanic political power. New Hispanic leaders are searching for strategies that will galvanize the diverse segments of the Hispanic community. Hispanic organizations are striving to politicize and mobilize the heretofore apolitical Hispanic population. Both groups recognize that the future of Hispanics in American politics is dependent upon their ability to get more Hispanics participating in the political process through registering and voting; forming bi-ethnic coalitions with other groups; electing more Hispanics to public office at all levels; making Hispanic concerns felt through lobbying in the political arena; and in formulating and implementing public policies that will enhance the situation of Hispanics in American life.

More than two centuries after the adoption of the Bill of Rights in the U.S. Constitution and over a century after the Civil War was fought to preserve those rights, many Americans are still struggling for equality and justice. Despite the historic civil rights laws passed by Congress in the 1960's and landmark decisions of the U.S. Supreme Court, some minority groups have struggled to carve their place in the mainstream of American life.

Hispanics--the fastest growing segment of the American population--have placed new and unique demands on American society. Earlier ethnic groups who came to America from northern, eastern and southern Europe in search of the American dream and the promise of security and freedom followed the path of assimilation toward their goals. To these earlier ethnics, becoming Americans meant shedding their cultural trappings in favor of a new American identity dominated by the English language and WASP ideals. As a result what has evolved in America is a conservative nativism wherein those groups which came before have challenged the legitimacy and worth of the new groups in becoming Americans.

Hispanics, like Indians and Asians, have sought those valued objectives without suffering the extinction of their cherished racial, linguistic or cultural identity. The challenge in American society in the wake of these new demands is whether the true meaning of the American creed--liberty, freedom and equality-- can be fulfilled through tolerance for these different languages and divergent cultural customs. Hispanics and the new ethnic groups will eventually be integrated into the American system and the true measure of the greatness of the American system will be seen only if the new concept of "Americans" will include those of Spanish origin as well as Anglo-Saxon.

Introduction

[1]See for example on Mexican-Americans: Joan Moore, Mexican Americans (Englewood Cliffs, N.J.: Prentice-Hall, 1976); Maurilio Vigil, Chicano Politics (Washington, D.C.: University Press of America, 1978); F. Chris Garcia and Rudy de la Garza, The Chicano Political Experience (North Scituate, Ma.: Duxbury Press, 1976). On Puerto Ricans, see: Anibal Molina, "Puerto Rican Americans: A Study in Diversity," in The Minority Report, ed. Anthony Dworkin (New York: Praeger, 1976); Joseph Fitzpatrick, Puerto Rican Americans (Englewood Cliffs, N.J.: Prentice-Hall, 1971); James Jennings and Monte Rivera, Puerto Rican Politics in Urban America (Westport, Ct.: Greenwood Press, 1984).

[2]See for example David Edwards, The American Political Experience (Englewood Cliffs, N.J.: Prentice-Hall, 1985), p. 429, and Steffen Schmidt et al., American Government and Politics Today (St. Paul: West Publishing Co., 1985), p. 139.

[3]A Population Reference Bureau study made the projections of Hispanic population growth. Lloyd Sherer, "Intelligence Report," Parade Magazine, September 10, 1983.

[4]"Basic Demographic and Economic Data on U.S. Hispanics," La Luz Magazine, August-September, 1980, p. 28.

[5]Page Smith, "From Masses to Peoplehood," Historical Reflections 1, No. 1 (June, 1974), pp. 134-35.

Chapter I, Hispanics In American Politics: A Theoretical Approach

[1]Walter Kantowicz, "Politics," Harvard Encyclopedia of American Ethnic Groups, Steven Thernstrom, et. al., eds. (Cambridge, Massachusetts: Harvard University Press, 1980), p. 806.

[2]Michael Levy and Marv Kramer, The Ethnic Factor (New York: Simon and Shuster, 1972), p. 12.

[3] Ibid., p. 11.

[4] See F. Chris Garcia and Rodolfo de la Garza, _The Chicano Political Experience_ (North Scituate, Ma.: Duxbury Press, 1977) and Joan Moore, _Mexican Americans_ (2nd ed.; Englewood Cliffs, N.J.: Prentice-Hall, 1976).

[5] In Michael B. Preston, _et. al._, _The New Black Politics_ (New York: Longman Publishing Co., 1982), p. xix.

Chapter II, Brief Sketches: Mexican-Americans, Cubans, Puerto Ricans and "Others"

[1] Don Juan de Onate, governor and _adelantado_ led 200 Spanish soldiers and their families into New Mexico in 1598 in what became the first permanent European settlement in what is now the United States.

[2] See Carey McWilliams, _North From Mexico_ (Philadelphia: J.B. Lippincott Company, 1949), p. 52.

[3] _The New American Encyclopedia_ (Washington, D.C.: The Publishers Agency, Inc., 1972), Vol. 11, pp. 4147-4148.

[4] Ibid., Vol. 4, pp. 1396-1399.

[5] See Daniel Yankelovich, Skelly and White, _Spanish USA: A Study of the Hispanic Market in the United States_. Study conducted for the SIN National Spanish Television Network, New York; (June, 1981), p. 4.

[6] Ibid.

[7] Ibid.

[8] Ibid.

[9] U.S. Bureau of the Census, "Condition of Hispanics in America Today," September, 1983.

[10] Population Reference Bureau, Inc., _Population Bulletin_, Vol 38, No 3, Washington, D.C., 1983.

[11] "Condition of Hispanics in America Today."

[12]Population Bulletin, op. cit.

[13]"Conditions of Hispanics in America Today."

Chapter III, The Hispanic Vote

[1]ABC News Polling Unit, "ABC News Poll, Year-end Wrapup," 1985.

[2]For such cross-ethnic voting comparisons see Walter Kantowicz, "Poltics," in Harvard Encyclopedia of American Ethnic Groups, op. cit., pp. 808-812.

[3]National Broadcasting Company, NBC News: Decision 84, General Election Results, New York, 1985.

[4]CBS News/New York Times Polls, National Election Day, 1984, "Hispanics vs. Other Voters."

[5]For a discussion of the Hispanic vote in New Mexico see Maurilio E. Vigil, "Chicano Voting Behavior," Chapter 7 in Chicano Politics (Washington, D.C.: University Press of America, 1978), pp. 306-358.

[6]Discussion of these Hispanic Congressmen and their constituency is provided in Chapter 4.

[7]U.S. Bureau of the Census, "Condition of Hispanics in America Today," September 13, 1983.

[8]See for example Tom Diaz, "Turning Numbers into Clout," Nuestro, Vol 7, No 10, (December, 1983), pp. 34-35.

[9]Robert Brischetto and Rodolfo O. de la Garza, The Mexican American Electorate: Political Participation and Ideology, Occasional Paper No 3 in The Mexican American Electorate Series (San Antonio: Southwest Voter Registration and Education Project, 1983).

[10]Ibid., p. 2.

[11]Ibid., p. 4.

[12]Ibid., p. 10.

[13]Ibid., p. 15.

[14]Ibid., p. 19-22.

[15]Douglas St. Angelo and Paul Puryear, "Fear, Apathy and Other Dimensions of Black Voting," in Michael B. Preston, et. al. eds,. The New Black Politics (New York: Longman Publishing Co., 1982), pp. 109-130.

Chapter IV, Hispanics in National Office

[1]See profile on "Jose Manuel Gallegos" in Maurilio E. Vigil, Los Patrones: Profiles of Hispanic Political Leaders in New Mexico History (Washington, D.C.: University Press of America, 1980), p. 41.

[2]The eight are Miguel A. Otero, Francisco Perea, J. Francisco Chavez, Trinidad Romero, Mariano Otero, Tranquilino Luna, Francisco Manzanares, and Pedro Perea. Jose M. Gallegos also served an additional term. See M. Vigil Los Patrones...

[3]Vigil, Los Patrones..., pp. 143-145.

[4]Ibid., p. 147.

[5]Ibid., pp. 126-27.

[6]See Maurilio Vigil and Roy Lujan, "Parallels In the Careers of Two Hispanic U.S. Senators," Occasional Paper Series, No 4, University of Texas at El Paso, Chicano Studies Publication Program, August, 1985.

[7]"Linda Chavez: Running Right," Impact: The Albuquerque Journal Magazine, September 2, 1986, pp. 4-9. Also Las Vegas Daily Optic, September 19, 1986.

[8]Profile on Congressman Gonzales is taken from a biographical sketch "Congressman Henry B. Gonzales," published by the Congressman's staff. Washington, D.C., 1981.

[9]"Biography of E. (Kika) de la Garza." Prepared by the Congressman's staff, Washington, D.C.

[10]"Congressman Manuel Lujan, Jr. - Biographical Data." Prepared by Congressman Lujan's staff, Washington, D.C., 1982.

[11]"Biographical Sketch: The Honorable Robert Garcia, Congressman (D-N.Y.)." Prepared by the Congressman's staff, Washington, D.C., 1982.

[12]For discussion of these elections see Maurilio Vigil, "Hispanics Gain Seats in the 98th Congress After Reapportionment," International Social Science Review Vol 59, No 1, (Winter, 1984), pp. 20-30.

[13]Congressional Quarterly and Weekly Report, October 13, 1984 and December 8, 1984.

[14]Stated in a pamphlet on "The History of the Congressional Hispanic Caucus." Washington, D.C.: Congressional Hispanic Caucus, 1981.

[15]A Guide to Hispanic Organizations (New York: Phillip Morris Public Affairs Dept., 1981), p. 22.

[16]Paul Weick, "Different Interest, Personalities Hurt Unity of Hispanic Caucus," Albuquerque Journal, December 18, 1983.

[17]Ibid.

[18]Ibid.

[19]See A Directory of Hispanic Appointees in the Carter Administration, 1980. Washington, D.C., 1980.

[20]Ibid.

[21]Facts on File, January 13, 1984.

Chapter V, Hispanics in Public Office-State and Local Levels

[1]For a more detailed discussion of this see Maurilio E. Vigil, "The Political Development of Hispanic New Mexicans," in The Hispanics of New Mexico: Essays on History and Culture (Bristol, Indiana: Wyndham Hall Press, 1984).

[2]See Maurilio E. Vigil, "Chicano Voting Behavior," in Chicano Politics (Washington, D.C.: University Press of America, 1978).

[3]See Maurilio E. Vigil, "Jerry Apodaca and the 1974 Gubernatorial Election in New Mexico: An Analysis," _AZTLAN: International Journal of Chicano Studies Research_, Vol 9 (1978), pp. 133-150.

[4]Vigil, "Chicano Voting Behavior," pp. 323-332 and 349-356.

[5]John Robertson, "Anaya Popularity at Low Ebb, Poll Shows," _Albuquerque Journal_, November 17, 1985. This poll conducted late in Anaya's third year in office showed the Governor receiving a 23.4 percent "favorable" and 55.8 percent "unfavorable" rating as as Governor.

[6]See Chapter 4.

[7]Vigil, _Chicano Politics_, pp. 205-206.

[8]See Chapter 6.

[9]Vigil, _Chicano Politics_, pp. 201-203.

[10]Ibid., pp. 219-243.

[11]_Who's Who in America_, 1984-1985, p. 133.

[12]For a discussion of this see Maurilio Vigil and Roy Lujan, "Parallels In the Careers of Two Hispanic U.S. Senators," _Occasional Paper Series_, No 4, University of Texas at El Paso, Chicano Studies Publication Program, August, 1985.

[13]See Maurilio E. Vigil, "Chicano Voting Behavior," _op. cit._, p. 324.

[14]For an in-depth discussion of this election see Maurilio E. Vigil, "The Election of Toney Anaya as Governor of New Mexico and Its Implications for Hispanics," _The Journal of Ethnic Studies_, Vol 12, No 2 (Summer, 1984), pp. 81-98.

[15]John Robertson, "Anaya Popularity at Low Ebb," _op. cit._

[16]See Irwin Ross, "Mayor Cisneros of San Antonio," _Reader's Digest_, (December, 1984), pp. 194-198.

[17]Ibid.

[18]Ibid.

[19] Jim Wood, "A Popular Mayor Pursues An Economic Development Agenda," _Nuestro_, Vol 8, No 8, (October, 1984), pp. 17-21.

[20] Ibid.

[21] Ibid.

[22] "Hispanic Power At the Polls," _Newsweek_, July 4, 1983, p. 23.

[23] Chip Martinez, "Federico Pena, Denver's First Hispanic Mayor," _Nuestro_ (August, 1983), p. 14.

[24] Ibid.

[25] "Pena's Open Style Draws Acclaim," _Rocky Mountain News_, October 2, 1983.

[26] Ibid.

[27] "Pena--1 Year Later: Still Imagining A Great City," _Denver Post_, June 10, 1984.

[28] Ibid.

[29] Personal letter written by Mayor Federico Pena to New Mexico Highlands University graduate student Jeffrey Ishmael, March 25, 1985.

[30] _Who's Who in America_, p. 1019.

[31] Jeff Ishmael, "Cisneros, Pena and Ferre: Case Studies of Three Hispanic Mayors." A Graduate Student Paper for Southwest Politics, New Mexico Highlands University, Spring, 1984.

[32] Much of this discourse is based on a series of telephone interviews with Miami Clerical Officers, Office of Public Information, City of Miami, October 30, 1985 and November 18, 1985.

[33] "Biographical Information on Raul L. Martinez, Mayor of Hialeah," City of Hialeah, Florida, 1985.

[34] "Bob Martinez, Mayor, City of Tampa, Florida." Biographical sketch published by Executive Offices, City of Tampa, Florida.

[35]Office of Public Information, Council of the City of New York, News Release containing biographical sketch of Councilman Fernando Ferrer.

[36]Office of Public Information, Council of the City of New York, News Release containing biographical sketch of Councilman Rafael Castaneira Colon.

[37]Office of Public Information, Council of the City of New York, News Release containing biographical sketch of Councilman Victor L. Robles.

[38]Rufus Browning, Dale Rogers Marshall and David H. Tubb, "Protest Is Not Enough: A Theory of Political Incorporation," P.S., Vol XIX, No 3, (Summer, 1986), pp. 516-581.

[39]Ibid.

[40]Raphe Sonnenstein, "Biracial Politics in Los Angeles," P.S., Vol XIX, No 3, (Summer, 1986), pp. 582-590.

[41]Ibid.

[42]Carlos Munoz and Charles Henry, "Rainbow Coalitions in Four Big Cities: San Antonio, Denver, Chicago and Philadelphia," P.S., Vol XIX, No 3, (Summer, 1986), pp. 598-609.

[43]Ibid.

[44]Christopher Warren, John Stack and John G. Corbett, "Minority Mobilization in an International City: Rivalry and Conflict in Miami," P.S., Vol XIX, No 3, (Summer, 1986), pp. 626-634.

[45]Ibid.

Chapter VI, Hispanic Organizations

[1]Edgar Litt, Ethnic Politics In America (Glenview, Illinois: Scott, Foresman and Co., 1970), p. 42.

[2]A "categoric group is any group to which a given label can be applied, such as the elderly, consumers, children. Every ethnic minority group is in a sense a

categoric group made up of diverse people who may or
may not identify with the label attached to them. A
categoric group differs from an organized pressure
group which actively lobbies government or interacts
with other groups in pursuit of objectives consistent
with the shared interest. The assumption is that a
categoric group must undergo some alteration before it
becomes a viable pressure group.

[3]Several scholars have identified these four
periods in the political development of Hispanics. See
for example Chapter 8 in Joan Moore and Alfredo
Cuellar, The Mexican Americans (Englewood Cliffs, New
Jersey: Prentice-Hall, 1970). Also Ralph C. Guzman,
"The Political Socialization of the Mexican-American
People," (Unpublished Ph.D. Dissertation, University of
California Los Angeles, 1970), pp. 196-197.

[4]For a more extensive discussion of these four
periods and examples of Hispanic organizations in each
period see Maurilio Vigil, "Ethnic Organizations Among
the Mexican Americans of New Mexico: A Political Perspective." Ph.D. Dissertation, University of New
Mexico, 1974.

[5]Ibid.

[6]Ibid.

[7]Mexican American Legal Defense and Education
Fund, MALDEF Newsletter, April, 1986.

[8]Vigil, "Ethnic Organization Among the Mexican
Americans of New Mexico..." op. cit.

[9]Much of the subsequent discussion and references
to Hispanic organizations, unless otherwise noted, are
taken from A Guide to Hispanic Organizations (New York:
Phillip Morris Public Affairs Dept., 1981). This
pamphlet was published for the Congressional Hispanic
Caucus. The categories have been established by this
writer for ease in discussion and analysis.

[10]Mexican American Legal Defense and Education
Fund, MALDEF Newsletter, April, 1986.

[11]Facts on File, November 26, 1985.

[12]Facts on File, November 26, 1985, December 10,
1985 and March 5, 1986.

[13]Vigil, "Ethnic Organizations Among the Mexican Americans..." op. cit.

[14]"Hispanic Catholic Conference Chronicles Expanding Role," Albuquerque Journal, August 18, 1985.

Chapter VII, Political Strategies and Prospects

[1]National Association of Latino Elected and Appointed Officials, 1984 National Roster of Hispanic Elected Officials (Washington, D.C.: NALEO Education Fund, 1984), p. xv.

[2]Ibid., p. xvi.

[3]Steve Padilla, "In Search of Hispanic Voters," Nuestro, August, 1983, p. 20.

ABOUT THE AUTHOR

Maurilio E. Vigl is Professor of Political Science at New Mexico Highlands University. He has degrees from New Mexico Highlands University (B.A., 1964 and M.A., 1966) and a Ph.D. from the University of New Mexico (1974). He is a member of the Western Political Science Association, the Western Social Science Association, Phi Kappa Phi (National Honorary) and Pi Gamma Mu (National Social Science Honorary).

His other books are Chicano Politics (1978), Los Patrones: Profiles of Hispanic Political Leaders In New Mexico History (1980) both published by University Press of America and The Hispanics of New Mexico: Essays on History and Culture (1984), by Wyndham Hall Press. He has contributed chapters to New Mexico Government (University of New Mexico Press, 1982) and Chicanos As We See Ourselves (University of Arizona Press, 1979).